In *Grace-Focused Optimism*, Pastor Charley Chase encounters the age-old problem of pessimism within the church and tackles it head on. With a pastor's heart, a scholar's mind, and a winning coach's motivational skills, Chase shines the light of truth into the dark corners of our misconceptions about life and redirects our thinking to the gospel of Christ. For anyone depressed, disheartened, or simply 'weary in well doing', this book offers genuine help and hope.

Ann M. Robertson
Editorial Consultant, Atlanta, Georgia

I have been in a men's bible study led by C. L. Chase for a long time. He has taught me—and a number of other Christian businessmen—that the only people on the face of this earth who have reason to be optimistic are Christians. I'm glad that Charley is sharing these truths with others in *Grace-Focused Optimism*. It's the best book I know for helping believers discover the principles for successful Christian living in a fallen world. *Grace-Focused Optimism* is a must read for any Christian wanting to know how to handle life well to God's glory.

Martin Wilson
Attorney at Law, Macon, Georgia

The premise of C. L. Chase's book, *Grace-Focused Optimism*, is that from beginning to end salvation is by God's grace. One does not simply begin the Christian life by grace but should depend on and focus on God's grace for all of life. In his own inimitable style, Dr. Chase coaches us on how to live by grace each moment of each day.

Joseph A. Pipa
President, Greenville Theological Seminary
Greenville, South Carolina

Lest you think that this is some positive thinking, self-help, repackaging of the Prosperity-gospel to produce a confidence in self, it's not. What it does do is change your thinking from 'Grace is God giving me the opposite of what I deserve' to 'Grace is God's governing determination to do me good in all of His dealings with me.' 'Being a Christian means that you're someone in whose life grace has the first and last word, everyday, all day long.' Dr. Chase's analogies are not hackneyed or trite but fresh and original. The book is solid and sound with Biblical and doctrinal support. I have been privileged to sit in the bleachers and see the demonstration of God's grace performed both in his life and ministry. He and *Grace-Focused Optimism* are trophies of God's amazing grace! To God be all the glory!

Ronald W. McKinney
Pastor, Educator, Dalton, Georgia

C. L. Chase's *Grace-Focused Optimism* is a charter for a truly happy Christianity. Years ago I had the privilege of worshiping in the church where Charley was the Pastor, enjoying his preaching. In a sense I got to watch, and benefit from, a live version of the book in Charley's ministry not only hearing his sermons but talking with him during the week about the sermon and the Christian life. Charley makes clear that the gospel of Christ is not just a set of ideas that one mentally accepts, but a life-changing dynamic for every day living. In Galatians 3:1-3 St. Paul says, 'O foolish Galatians! Who has bewitched you that you should not obey the truth, before whose eyes Jesus Christ was clearly portrayed among you as crucified? This only I want to learn from you: Did you receive the Spirit by the works of the law, or by the hearing of faith?—Are you so foolish? Having begun in the Spirit, are you now being made perfect by the flesh?' And in 5:1 he says, 'Stand fast therefore in the liberty by which Christ has made us free, and do not be entangled again with a yoke of bondage.'

I am delighted that Charley is now making the fruit of his ministry available to a wider audience.

Daniel R. Morse
Bishop, Diocese of the Central States
The Reformed Episcopal Church

Grace is a such a commonly used word in the church that it may at times lose its significance. So when someone unpacks it with a fresh perspective, an angle that captures it in a heart satisfying sense, we take notice. Charley Chase does this in *Grace-Focused Optimism*. Here you will find the power of grace that really does change everything in your world. You will be refreshed in every way because, as Charley delights to say, 'God is determined to get glory from you by giving grace to you.' Scripture tells us that those whom God foreknew, he predestined to be conformed to the likeness of his Son (Romans 8:29). *Grace-Focused Optimism* will spur you on towards conformity to Jesus, and in so doing will empower you with a sense of being borne along on the wings of grace.

Dominic Aquila
New Geneva Seminary, Colorado Springs, Colorado

Dr. Charley L. Chase will not let you forget that God Almighty loves you and is on your side. He gently reminds us, through his Grace-Focused Optimism conferences, gfoministries.com website, and, above all, his book, *Grace Focused Optimism*, that you can't help being a joyful, blessed Christian if you focus on God's grace. His book is a treasure and resource that will lift your heart. I highly recommend it!

John Carenen
Author, *Signs of Struggle* and *A Far Gone Night*

'Grace' is perhaps the most used word in the evangelical vocabulary. However, it is not as well understood as it should be and needs to be. Charley L. Chase has written a biblical, passionate and personal exposition of what the Bible means by grace. It is biblical because Charley understands exactly what the grace of God is, his undeserved, unmerited kindness to judgement deserving sinners. It is passionate because Charley rightly grasps that grace is not simply a gospel truth, it is a gospel glory, a glory every Christian needs to be mastered by. It is personal because Charley has himself been mastered by the grace of God in Jesus Christ. There is an infectious 'grace-focused optimism' that pulses through this book. Read it and catch the infection.

Ian Hamilton
Associate Minister
Smithton-Culloden Free Church of Scotland, Inverness

When you view the world, what do you see? It is so easy to be discouraged, depressed, and pessimistic. Things seem to be getting worse, and it is natural to see the glass half-empty rather than half-full. C. L. Chase's book *Grace-Focused Optimism* will help you to refocus your life, and to see things as they really are! For a Christian, optimism is not a product of a 'Pollyanna' mindset, but of a God-created faith that's centered in all that the grace of the Gospel supplies for day-to-day living. Read this book and see how.

Paul Kooistra
Former Coordinator of The Mission to the World Committee
Presbyterian Church in America

Grace-Focused Optimism reveals a deep and rich understanding of God's grace to us in Jesus. It is concise, well written, full of Scripture and apt metaphors that make it a pleasure to read. It is also good, sanctifying food for the hungry Christian. Open, read, and bask more deeply in God's determination to be good to you through His dear Son. A must read!

David Jussely
Adjunct Professor Reformed Theological Seminary, Jackson Associate Pastor, First Presbyterian Church, Hattiesburg, Mississippi

If you have picked up this book looking for an academic theological treatise, I would recommend you find another. There are lots of good ones out there! But, if you are interested in how good theology impacts your soul then I highly recommend you read it!

Grace-Focused Optimism is Charley Chase at his best, ministering experimental Christianity to the hearts of God's people. In this book rests forty-five years of pastoral wisdom, insight, and experience. If you need encouragement, if you need a fresh sense of the nearness of Jesus Christ, if you desire to grow and mature in a biblical approach to the Christian life, then don't put this book down. There are not lots of these out there.

My delight in recommending this book rests primarily in a cherished 35 year friendship with the author and his family and the fact that as a former Elder and Church Planter I long to see God's people living with the optimism about God that grace gives us reason to have.

Kent Thompson
Ruling Elder, Reformed Baptist Church

A multitude of struggling souls stand to be blessed richly by Pastor Chase's *Grace-Focused Optimism*. Mine surely was. I first read it during a wilderness period in my life, and it proved a timely refreshment to my spirit. Each chapter enabled me to grasp a deeper understanding of the grace of God and behold more of the glory of His Only Begotten Son. Put this book on the top of your reading list! I am sure that your heart will be strengthened as your understanding of God's grace is enlarged.

Alan Lutz
Pastor of Crystal Cove Community Church, Palm Harbor, Florida
Haiti Project Director for MINTS International Seminary

GRACE-FOCUSED

Optimism

C. L. CHASE

CHRISTIAN
FOCUS

10 9 8 7 6 5 4 3 2 1

Copyright © C. L. Chase 2017

paperback ISBN 978-1-5271-0042-8

epub ISBN 978-1-5271-0081-7

mobi ISBN 978-1-5271-0082-4

First published in 2017

by

Christian Focus Publications Ltd,

Geanies House, Fearn, Ross-shire,

IV20 1TW, Scotland.

www.christianfocus.com

A CIP catalogue record for this book is available from the British Library.

Cover design by Kent Jensen

Printed and bound by
Bell and Bain, Glasgow

Contents

To Sue
Your love, faithfulness, and mercy keep me mindful
that God's grace IS amazing.

INTRODUCTION

'The most basic battle of our life is the battle to believe in the living God, and not to allow our heart to become an evil heart of unbelief. Because if unbelief in God gets the upper hand in our life, then the result can be a hardening that makes us unwilling to repent and thus cuts us off from the grace of God … Unbelief is the root and essence of evil. All our sinning grows out of unbelief in the living God and what he has said to us in Scripture.'

John Piper[1]

It's about you and grace. If you're like me, the first question you ask before you commit to reading a book is 'What's it about?' Well, here's my answer: this book is about you and grace. Specifically, it's about you living as a Grace-Focused Optimist. I ask you not to be put off by the noun 'optimist.' As I seek to show in the following chapters, a Christian is an optimist in the sense that he or she knows that grace

1. John Piper, www.desiringgod.org/sermons/battling-the-unbelief-of-anxiety

means God is *always* up to his or her good. God always *intends* a believer's good (Gen. 50:20); always *gives* good to a believer (Matt. 7:11); and, always *works* all things to a believer's good (Rom. 8:28). A Grace-Focused Optimist is someone who lives in, with, and by the assurance, 'God is always up to my good.'

To live as a Grace-Focused Optimist you'll have to go through paradigm shifts. A paradigm is a way of seeing something. A paradigm shift is a change in the way you see that something.[2]

My favorite paradigm shift happens in the movie *To Kill a Mockingbird*. Jem Finch is the son of widower Atticus Finch, a lawyer in the small town of Macomb, Alabama. Jem loves Atticus but doesn't respect him because Atticus won't play football with the Methodists. What kind of Southern father doesn't play football, for heaven's sake? But Jem's view of Atticus changes the day he and his sister Scout see a dog wobbling down their street like a drunk man. They dash inside and tell housekeeper Calpurnia. Calpurnia takes a look and immediately calls Attitcus. 'Mr Finch, you'd better come quick. There's a rabid dog comin' down the street.' Soon a black Model T pulls up to the house. Sherriff Heck Tate steps out the driver's side with a rifle; Atticus gets out of the passenger's seat. 'He needs to be shot Mr Finch,' Heck says.

---

2. 'The word *paradigm* comes from the Greek. It was originally a scientific term, and is more commonly used today to mean a model, theory, perception, assumption, or frame of reference. In the more general sense, it's the way we 'see' the world—not in terms of our visual sense of sight, but in terms of perceiving, understanding, interpreting.... paradigm shifts move us from one way of seeing the world to another.... If we want to make significant, quantum change, we need to work on our basic paradigms.' Stephen R. Covey, *The 7 Secrets of Highly Effective People*, (New York: Simon & Shuster, 1989), pp. 23; 30-31.

'Shoot him, Heck,' Atticus urges. Handing Atticus the rifle Tate says, 'No, you shoot him Mr Finch.' Atticus takes it as nimbly as a surgeon receiving a scalpel, lifts it to his shoulders, aims, squeezes the trigger, *BLAM!* The dog's dangerous dementia is over. The camera pans to Jem. His eyes are Frisbee wide. Heck Tate looks at him. 'What's the matter, son? Didn't you know your daddy is the best shot in Macomb County?' No, Jem didn't know. But he does now. And now it doesn't matter whether Atticus plays football with the Methodists. Now Atticus is the kind of dad every boy wants, a dad who can drop a rabid dog with a single rifle shot from a distance of two football fields. Jem's paradigm has shifted.

To live as a Grace-Focused Optimist you'll have to go through three grace paradigm shifts. The *first and fundamental* grace paradigm shift is a shift about *how* God wants you to live as a Christian. You undergo this shift when you realize God wants you to choose to live with the grace-governed attitude of optimism about Him. Undergoing this paradigm shift depends on experiencing two other shifts. The *second* grace paradigm shift is a shift about *heart* grace (God's favor). You need your *understanding* of grace changed from 'Grace is God giving me the opposite of what I deserve' to 'Grace is God's governing determination to do me good in all of His dealings with me.' The *third* grace paradigm shift you'll have to undergo is a shift about *hand* grace (God's help)[3]. You need to change from *using* grace now and then to using it every day, all day long, to

---

3. J. I. Packer, *God's Words*, (Downers Grove, Illinois: InterVarsity Press, 1981), p. 98. *Heart* grace is God's unmerited favor, seen, for example, in Noah, Genesis 6:8. *Hand* grace is God's assistance of any kind, seen, for example, in Paul's thorn experience, 2 Corinthians 12:9-10.

stay optimistic about God. This involves developing a set of habits that will help you continuously focus on grace. (If the idea of 'using' grace sounds odd, it indicates how much you need to make this shift.) When you go through these paradigm shifts you will be able to live as the Grace-Focused Optimist God wants you to be.

My preaching professor in seminary was Richard Allen Bodey. Mr Bodey was the faculty's Bear Bryant. He would have been that at any school fortunate enough to have him. He was that good as a teacher and that scary. Students coming through his classes were like Bear's 'Junction Boys': survivors[4] – and grateful for the experience. Mr Bodey made us better preachers. The main reason for this was his Bear-like, non-negotiable, 'My way or the highway' philosophy about preparing sermons.

In 1922 Winston Churchill gave future Prime Minister Harold Macmillan wise counsel after Macmillan's first speech in Parliament. 'Harold,' Churchill told him, 'everyone in the gallery was saying, "Young Macmillan is giving his maiden address." And they asked, "What is it about?" Harold, if people can't say in one sentence what the speech is about, it's a speech not worth delivering.'[5]

Mr Bodey would have agreed and added that the best way for an audience to say in one sentence what a speech is about is for the speaker to say it for them in one sentence. He called this *Reader's Digest* lean summary sentence a

---

4. 'The Junction boys' is the name given to Bryant's first Texas A & M football team. They got this name from enduring his grueling preseason workout in a small Texas town.

5. James Humes, *The Sir Winston Method*, (New York: William Morrow and Company, 1991), p. 45.

'proposition.' He assured us we weren't ready to preach a sermon until we had a proposition governing our entire message as ruthlessly as a despotic king and as prominently as an engagement ring diamond. Because of Mr Bodey's drilling, I think propositionally, I preach propositionally, and I write propositionally. So, though this is a book not a sermon, it has a proposition. This proposition summarizes the paradigm shifts you need to make to live as a Grace-Focused Optimist. Here is my single sentence summary of everything I've got to say. *God wants you to live as a Grace-Focused Optimist by understanding and using the truth that, through Jesus, He is determined to get glory from you by giving grace to you.* Seven soul-stirring convictions are embedded in this proposition. Let's glance at each.

1. Conviction one is, *God is determined to get glory from you.* The Bible is the original *Purpose-Driven Life* book. It stresses that life itself – creation and all that is, including my life and yours – is purpose-driven. It's driven by God's purpose. His invincible purpose is the sun in the solar system of everything He does. He makes this sun shine with noonday brightness in His Word by telling us plainly and repeatedly what He is up to with everything and everyone. God says He is out to glorify Himself by demonstrating His greatness to all the angels and all mankind.[6] Your life, like

---

6. 'God's zeal for his fame to be spread bursts out in the Scriptures again and again.' John Piper, *The Pleasures of God*, Portland, Oregon: Multnomah, Press, 1991), p. 112. The Bible backs up Piper's boast: See, for example, Isaiah. 66:19, Romans. 9:22-23, Romans. 11:36 and Ephesians. 1:6, 12, 14. For a carefully articulated exegesis of a key biblical passage regarding God's zeal for his glory, Romans 9:22-23, see Jay Adams, *The Grand Demonstration*, (Santa Barbara, California: East Gate Publishers, 1991).

everything else, is the venue for His display of how great He is. Understand that and you have the GPS you need to travel safely, sanely and cheerfully through life's chronic challenges.

2. Conviction two is the fact that *God's way of getting glory from you as a Christian is by giving grace to you.* The first of Campus Crusade for Christ's 'Four Spiritual Laws' is 'God loves you and has a wonderful plan for your life.' Christian, that's what the Bible says to you. And it tells you His wonderful plan for your life is a Grace Plan. Grace is God's glory strategy for you. Giving grace *to* you is how He's going to get glory *from* you. This isn't a peripheral strategy or one among many plays in the Lord's glory playbook. It's His eternal, exclusive, and invincible strategy for getting glory from you. *Eternal*, because before the foundation of the world He chose to get glory from you by giving grace to you.[7] *Exclusive*, because all of His dealings with you from start to finish have been, are, and will be grace dealings.[8] *Invincible*, because having begun a good work in you He will bring it to perfection.[9] Grace is the sum and substance of God's handling of your life. Grace's fingerprints are on everything that happens to you (and, let it be said, what does *not* happen to you!). You live and move and have your being in grace. You're a 'vessel of mercy prepared beforehand for glory.'[10] This is what your Bible means when it tells you that you are 'under grace'[11] and 'stand in grace.'[12]

---

7. Ephesians. 1:4-5.

8. Ephesians 1:3-14; 2:1-12.

9. Philippians 1:6.

10. Romans 9:23.

11. Romans 6:14.

12. Romans 5:1-2.

Being a Christian means that you're someone in whose life grace has the first and last word, every day, all day long.[13]

3. Conviction three is *God wants you to understand what grace is.* Barry Shealy is the Assistant Headmaster at the school I serve as chaplain.[14] A few years ago he gave the most memorable Elementary School chapel talk our students have heard. Barry told the several hundred 1st-6th graders present that day that 'God is good – all the time.' You can walk into any class of students who heard that talk and say, 'God is good' and they'll immediately chorus back 'All the time!' God's all-the-time goodness is the essence of grace. Saying that God is going to get glory from you by giving grace to you is saying that God's strategy for getting glory from you is by being good to you – all the time![15] In other words, grace means God is 100 per cent for you 100 per cent of the time. No other concept of grace does justice to Paul's assurance: 'If God be for us who (then) can be against us?'[16] Change the 'If' to 'Since' (which is Paul's

---

13. 'It is grace at the beginning, grace at the end. So that when you and I come to lie upon our deathbeds, the one thing that should comfort and help and strengthen us there is the thing that helped us at the beginning. Not what we have been, not what we have done, but the grace of God in Jesus Christ our Lord. The Christian life starts with grace, it must continue with grace, it ends with grace. Grace, wondrous grace. "By the grace of God I am what I am." "Yet not I, but the grace of God which was with me."' *D. Martyn Lloyd-Jones: Letters 1919-1981*, (Edinburgh: The Banner of Truth Trust, 1994), p. 237.

14. First Presbyterian Day School, Macon, Georgia.

15. I shall argue all the way through this book that by 'good' God doesn't mean cash but character; not health but holiness. God's definition of good, according to Romans 8:28-30, is bringing us to perfect and permanent happiness by making us perfectly and permanently like Jesus Christ spiritually and physically.

16. Romans 8:31 (KJV).

point) and you get his drift. God's determination to do you good isn't on and off again like a teenage romance. God's determination to do you good is always on; it governs your life 24/7; it never dozes, never goes on vacation, never takes a holiday.[17] You understand grace when you understand grace is God's determination to do you good, only good, and nothing but good, every day, all day long.

4. Conviction four is *God wants you to use grace every day.* Grace is a car key not a spare tire. It's not for sitting in your trunk until a flat tire experience; it's for carrying around in the pocket of your heart, ready for use each and every day, all day long. Triumphing believers from Abraham to Zinzendorf have *used* grace to savor and serve God and find in Jesus the abundant life of purpose, passion, peace, pleasure, power, and productivity. They have used grace to live as Grace-Focused Optimists. God wants you to do the same.[18]

5. Conviction five is *God wants you to live as an optimist no matter what's going on in your life.*[19] Football calls it

---

17. Psalm 23:6. 'Typically lost, we're always being escorted in the right direction; often perplexed, we're always on the right track. A. W. Tozer said boldly, 'The man or woman who is wholly and joyously surrendered to Christ cannot make a wrong choice.' He means, of course, that our eternal destiny is not riding on our next decision. No choice that we make is final or ultimately fatal. We may take the oddest path through the wilderness, but we can be assured of this fact: every day, whether we know it or not, we're being led along the path that leads us *home.*' David Roper, *Psalm 23: The Song of a Passionate Heart*, (Nashville, Tennessee: Discovery House Publishers, 1994), p. 114. Emphasis Roper's.

18. 2 Corinthians 12:9-10; Hebrews 4:14-16.

19. Again, I ask you not to be put off by the term 'optimism.' While it isn't a biblical term (neither is, for example, 'Trinity'), it's the best word I know to express the twin grace concepts of *hope* (what God has in store for us in the

momentum. A team's down by three touchdowns in the championship game. It's the start of the 4th Quarter. Nothing has worked for the home team so far. The offense is stagnant; the defense out to lunch. Then a punt is recovered on the opponent's 2-yard line. The next play the QB breaks the plane on a sneak. Touchdown!!! Coach holds up two fingers signaling 'We're going for 2!' The play works beautifully. Eight points have been scored in thirty seconds. Suddenly the sideline turns from morgue to Mardi Gras. Coaches' frowns bloom into smiles as they greet players trotting off the field with 'Way to go!' fist pumps. The kicking team's strapping on their helmets while sprinting to the 40-yard line. Fans are high fiving each other. What's going on? Everyone's suddenly thinking 'We can win this game!' What's happened? Momentum's wind has shifted. It's now blowing for the good guys, unfurling their sails, making them move like a schooner. What is momentum? It's rejuvenated, resurrected, freshly surging *optimism*. It's the belief you *can* succeed, you *can* make it, you *can* win. And you *will*! Christian man, believing woman, that's the kind of optimism God wants you to have as His child. Read these words and tell me what you'd call them: 'I can do all things through Christ which strengtheneth me … Nothing can separate us from the love of God in Jesus Christ … For he has said, "I will never leave you nor forsake you." So we may boldly say, "the Lord is my helper and I will not fear

---

future) and *help* (what God is willing to do for us in the present). As I seek to show, this optimism isn't due to temperament or circumstances. Its source isn't 'positive thinking' or unrealistic naiveté. Nor is it confidence in ourselves or in any other human being. It's God-centered optimism: what I call Grace-Focused Optimism. In other words, it's optimism *about God*. It's optimism that expects God to do for us all the good He graciously promises.

what man shall do to me.'"[20] If this isn't optimism, I don't know what it is. These verses demonstrate the rousing, rollicking, renewing, replenishing and reenergizing kind of optimism that ought to characterize your Christianity all the time. Notice, not *even* in your hard times; *especially* in your hard times. This is the kind of optimism God wants you to have no matter what's going on in your life.

6. Conviction six is *God wants you to live*. Paul Little says some people see God as a celestial Scrooge. He is bending over the balcony of heaven, searching for people having a good time. Why? So he can point a judgmental finger at them and say, 'You cut that out!'[21] I wish this were a caricature of believers. It isn't. Too many of us look at our heavenly Father through these bleak eyes. Too many of us see Him as a highway patrol God, hiding behind a billboard, radar gun pointed, hoping to catch us speeding so he can write us a ticket. Is this too harsh a judgment? I put it to your own conscience: would someone look at your Christianity and say, 'Wow! I want what that person has!'? Are you like George Whitefield? Someone said of him, 'Mr Whitefield was so cheerful he tempted me to become a Christian.'[22] Are you an advertisement for the Gospel? Are you enjoying God every day, all day long? Are you meeting life's challenges with Hebrews 11 calmness, courage, and confidence? God wants you to be able to say 'Yes!' to each of those questions. That's

---

20. Philippians 4:13 (KJV); Romans 8:38-39; Hebrews 13:5-6.

21. http:/bible.org/article/discerning-will-of-God

22. Leonard Ravenhill, *George Whitefield: Portrait of a Revival Preacher.* http://www.ravenhill.org/whitefield.htm

what His grace is all about. It's out to help you *LIVE* the abundant life Jesus came to give you.[23]

7. Conviction seven is it's *through Jesus* that God does this. After Sadhu Sundar Singh became a Christian he was asked by a Hindu college professor what he found in Christianity that Hinduism couldn't give him. 'I have Christ' Singh said. The professor nodded and said, 'Yes, I know, but what particular principle or doctrine have you found that you did not have before?' Singh said, 'The particular thing I have found is Christ.'[24] Jesus *is* the 'particular thing' of Christianity. He is this in God the Father's eyes. He is this in every believer's eyes. *And the particular thing about Jesus is His cross.* So, 'through Jesus' is shorthand for 'through Jesus crucified.' It's through Jesus that God gives grace to us and gets glory from us.[25] In fact, grace is all the good God is to us and does for us through Jesus.[26] It's through Jesus that God keeps His promises.[27] It's through Jesus that God secures for us everything necessary for us to live for Him in this life and with Him in the next.[28]

---

23. John 10:10.

24. John R. W. Stott, *The Incomparable Christ* (Downers Grove, IL, 2001), p. 16.

25. 'God and the cross (are) inextricably interrelated.' Their interrelation is that of glory and grace. Jesus' cross 'is the means of grace by which God is known' and 'the crucified Jesus is now the exalted Lord and hence the glory of God.' Michael J. Gorman, *Cruciformity: Paul's Narrative Spirituality of the Cross* (Grand Rapids, Michigan: William B. Eerdmans Publishing Company, 2001), pp. 9; 17; 25.

26. Romans 3:21 through Romans 11:36.

27. This is the theme of the Gospel of Matthew. Paul makes the same point in 2 Corinthians 1:20.

28. 2 Corinthians 5:18-19; John 19:30; Colossians 1:19-20.

It's through Jesus that God elects us.[29] It's through Jesus that God calls us.[30] It's through Jesus that God gives us saving faith.[31] It's through Jesus that God justifies us.[32] It's through Jesus that God adopts us.[33] It's through Jesus that God sends the Holy Spirit to live in us.[34] It's through Jesus that God provides all our need.[35] It's through Jesus that God works all things together for our good.[36] It's through Jesus that God preserves us for His coming kingdom.[37] *What's true for grace is also true for glory.* It's through Jesus that God glorifies Himself and gets glory from us.[38] It's through Jesus that we offer God acceptable spiritual sacrifices that bring Him honor.[39] It's through Jesus that the God-glorifying fruit of growth in love for Him and others is produced.[40] It's through Jesus that we exalt God by praising and thanking Him for hearing our prayers and intervening in our lives by granting us power to obey Him gladly, resist the devil, endure trial, witness boldly, and live an abundant life.[41] In sum, it's through Jesus that God blesses us in the sense of

---

29. Ephesians 1:4.

30. 1 Corinthians 1:2; Ephesians 2:1-7.

31. Ephesians 2:8-10; 2 Peter 1:1.

32. Romans 5:1 and 8:1.

33. John 20:17; Galatians 4:6.

34. Galatians 4:7.

35. Philippians 4:19.

36. Romans 8:28-30.

37. 2 Peter 1:3-6; Romans 8:35ff.

38. John 17:1-5; Ephesians 1:3-14, especially verses 3, 6, 12, and 14.

39. 1 Peter 2:5.

40. John 15:1-11; Philippians 1:8-11.

41. John 14:13; Ephesians 5:20; Ephesians 1:17-22; Romans 6:1-14; Luke 22:31-34; Matthew 28:16-20; Acts 2:14-41; 2 Timothy 4:16-17; John 10:10.

doing us His best good and it's through Jesus that we bless God in the sense of glorifying Him. The puritan John Flavel ended many of his sermons with the words, 'Blessed be God for Jesus Christ.' Amen. We will spend eternity blessing God for Jesus as we revel in the wonder of God getting glory from us by giving grace to us *through Jesus*.

Here's grace's bottom line. Being a Christian isn't first and foremost about you and your salvation; it's first and foremost about God and how He is determined to get glory from you. And for you as a Christian, the set-your-toe-to-tapping and your heart-to-racing wonder is that God chooses to get glory from you by giving grace to you through His beloved Son Jesus. That's God's glory strategy for you. God's glory strategy is a grace strategy. Grasp that, learn to focus on it, and you'll make the paradigm shift God wants you to make and begin living as a Grace-Focused Optimist.

That's the message of this book. It's a message about grace and you because it's a message about how God is determined to get glory from you by giving grace to you.

We turn now to paradigm shift one, The Grace Paradigm. Chapter one is entitled, '*To and Through: How God Changed My Paradigm.*' It may surprise you to find that though this is about grace and *you* I begin with grace and *me*. I begin this way because of two things Grace-Focused Optimism gives me. First, it gives me the courage to tell you the truth about how I lived a Methuselah long time without understanding and using grace in my everyday living. I call this failure 'the grace problem of living a grace-minimizing life.' It's not overdramatizing to say I was the foremost grace-minimizer among the Lord's people. And it's not joining Satan as an accuser of Christians to say that years of serving as a pastor and chaplain make me believe this spiritual malady is as common among believers as an allergy to dust. Maybe you aren't a grace-minimizer. Maybe you are. Reading my story can help you decide. Second, the fact that God is making me a Grace-Focused Optimist gives me confidence He can do the same for you if you need it. Years ago I read a story of a poor woman who was healed of a life-burdening sickness by a brilliant doctor. When she told him she couldn't pay he told her, 'Sure you can. Just tell everyone how sick you were and that I'm the one who healed you. That'll be pay enough because my success with you will bring me plenty of paying patients.' I'm trying to do something similar in telling you of God's success with me. Am I everything I ought to be? No. But I'm learning to live every day, all day long as a Grace-Focused Optimist. And the One Who is helping me has the will and skill to help you.

So, let's look at why I must begin this story about grace and you with the story of grace and me.

Paradigm Shift I

1

The Grace Paradigm
Four Facts About Grace and Optimism About God

'To be sure, there have always been some who have found the thought of grace so overwhelmingly wonderful that they could never get over it. Grace has become the constant theme of their talk and prayers. They have written hymns about it, some of the finest – and it takes deep feeling to produce a good hymn. They have fought for it, accepting ridicule and loss of privilege if need be as the price of their stand ...With Paul, their testimony is, 'By the grace of God I am what I am' (1 Cor. 15:10), and their rule of life is, 'I do not frustrate the grace of God' (Gal. 2:21 KJV). *But many church people are not like this.* They may pay lip service to the idea of grace, but there they stop. Their conception of grace is not so much debased as nonexistent. *The thought means nothing to them; it does not touch their experience at all.* Talk to them about the church's heating, or last year's accounts, and they are with you at once; but speak to them about the realities to which the word *grace* points, and their attitude is one of deferential blankness. They do not accuse you of talking nonsense; they do not doubt that your words have meaning; but they feel that, whatever it is you are talking about, it is beyond them, and the longer they have lived without it the surer they are that at their stage of life they do not really need it.'

J. I. Packer[1]

To and Through – How God Shifted My Paradigm

Since *Grace-Focused Optimism* argues that many Christians need to make a paradigm shift of epic proportions, I think it's imperative to begin by sharing how God shifted my paradigm and is helping me live as a Grace-Focused Optimist.

Like so many of God's best gifts, the gold of Grace-Focused Optimism was dug from the mine of personal crisis. Like so many crises, mine was vocational. Like so many vocational crises, mine was Tsunami strong. Like so many Christians in a vocational crisis, I didn't handle it well. I allowed it to bring me to debilitating discouragement.

I had not been a stranger to discouragement. Just the opposite. I was characterized by what John Piper calls 'emotional fragility.' Emotionally fragile people 'are easily broken … pout and mope easily … are easily disheartened, and …have little capacity for surviving and thriving in the face of criticism and opposition.'[2] That was a *Reader's Digest* summary of much of my life.

---

1. J. I. Packer, *Knowing God*, (Downers Grove, Illinois: InterVarsity Press, 1973), pp. 128-129. Emphases added in the two italicized sentences.

2. John Piper, *Brothers, We Must Not Mind a Little Suffering: Meditations on the Life of Charles Simeon* (Desiring God Ministries, printed paper, April 15, 1989).

This fragility haunted me from childhood to the borders of old age. Becoming a Christian didn't change this. Even as a believer, I continued breaking easier than a child's soap bubble bursts. Pouting, moping, sulking, and discouragement plagued me like flies besieging cattle on a hot August day.

Then came the vocational crisis that plunged me into a 'dark, drizzly November in my soul.' I was demoralized and dysfunctional. I ate little and slept a lot. It was the emotional equivalent of being buried alive.

The Tsunami moved through. The sun shone and the birds sang again. But my beach was littered with the post-storm debris of a hard question: why hadn't my Christianity helped me? I had cried, 'I'm drowning' but the lifeguard sat on his perch as though deaf. My Christianity seemed more like the priest and Levite than the Good Samaritan. No detective chasing a serial killer was more determined than I was to solve my mystery.

I knew the problem wasn't with Christianity. Paul's grasp of Jesus enabled him to sing in a dungeon at midnight while locked in stocks and bleeding from a scourging. Stephen's grasp of Jesus enabled him to forgive his murderers. Thousands of lesser-known believers have found their grasp of Jesus enabling them to be more than conquerors over disaster, disease, and death. But my grasp of Jesus was an empty river when my Goliath challenged. Why?

C. S. Lewis was helped by a man he called 'The Great Knock.' He was an unbeliever named William Kirkpatrick. I'm no Lewis but like him an unbeliever helped me. His name is Dr. Martin Seligman. He's a psychologist. His help came in the form of an idea he calls 'explanatory style.'[3]

By our explanatory style, Seligman means the way we *explain* our negative experiences to ourselves. He says we're mistaken when we think that we're down because a particular problem has taken us hostage. What gets us down isn't the problem but the way we *think* and *talk to ourselves* about it.

An explanatory style has several characteristics. It's *mental* in the sense that it's our opinion about our negative experiences. We see them as roses or thorns, friends or foes, obstacles or opportunities, nuisances or necessities.

An explanatory style is *universal*. Like DNA, everyone has one. Everyone has a way of thinking about negative experiences. Maybe, like me, you didn't know you had one. But you do.

An explanatory style is *dictatorial*. It governs our response to the problem we're facing. This is what makes it so important. It's either penicillin knocking out infection or a diseased lymphatic system spreading it. How you explain your problems to yourself controls how you handle them.

An explanatory style is *habitual*. By repetition, we've so ingrained a way of thinking about our negative experiences that it's our default response. Unless we intentionally work to change our explanatory style, we will think today about our problems the same way we thought five years ago and five months ago and five days ago. And thinking the same way, we'll respond the same way.

---

3. Martin E. P. Seligman, *Helplessness* (New York: W. H. Freeman and Company, 1975), pp. xx-xxxii.

An explanatory style is *discoverable*. We can find out what ours is by eavesdropping on what we say to ourselves when problems come.

An explanatory style is *changeable*. Because it's a way of thinking, it's not the mental equivalent of inoperable cancer or an irreversible paralysis. Since we can change the way we think we can change our explanatory style.

As I thought and prayed about this I realized that while Seligman didn't use the word 'paradigm' that's what he was talking about. The way I think and talk about my problems flows from what I think problems are. What I think my problems are is my way of seeing a problem. And how I see a problem is a paradigm.

This was Copernican for me. Suddenly things made sense. Why had I so mishandled my crisis? Because of my explanatory style. It was the way I thought and talked about my problem that was the drowning swimmer bringing me down. Why did I think and talk this way? Because of the way I looked at my problem. My failure was a paradigm failure.

The moment I saw this the game was afoot. I was a Christian. What was the Christian paradigm for problems? How was a Christian to think and talk about them? In other words, what is the Christian explanatory style for the difficulties we face? Only one book could answer this question. I began searching the Bible, interrogating it for the answer the way a detective does his prime suspect.

The Bible's answer came in the form of a single word: grace. As I read what God says about grace I came to see that my problem wasn't something wrong with my grasp of Jesus. My problem was the fact that I didn't understand or know how to use every day, all day long, Jesus' grasp of me. In other words, I had a grace problem. I have since come to see that my grace problem was my failure to live by the Grace Paradigm.

The Grace Paradigm can be put this way: *God wants us to choose to live with the grace-governed attitude of optimism about Him.* This paradigm is a priority, perspective, and preference, opening the door to pleasures we otherwise won't experience. It's a *priority* in the sense that God wants His children to live grace-governed lives. It's a *perspective* in the sense that living a grace-governed life means living with an attitude of optimism about God. It's a *preference* in the sense that living the grace-governed life of optimism about God is a choice. It's a choice that must be made again and again, every day, all day long. When we begin living by the Grace Paradigm, we begin experiencing *pleasures* we can only find in grace. These are the best pleasures imaginable.

I discovered that I hadn't been living by the Grace Priority. Please don't misunderstand. For years I had preached grace. I had sung about grace. But functionally I was *a grace-minimizing Christian.* Like a person looking through the wrong end of field glasses and seeing everything reduced in size, I saw grace as much smaller than it is. My definition of grace was the microscopic 'Grace is God giving us what we don't deserve.' My use of grace was small, too. I made decisions, fought discouragement, and handled trials without asking, 'How does grace help me with this?'

I wasn't characterized by the Grace Perspective either. Just the opposite. I lived with the pessimistic DNA of Jacob. Hearing from his sons what seemed to be bad news about their trip to Egypt, the patriarch lamented, 'All these things are against me.[4] This unbelieving pessimism contradicts the robust, 'all things for good,' perspective of optimism Romans 8:28 urges us to have about who and what God is to us in Christ by grace. It demonstrates itself in chronic complaining, debilitating discouragement, and lukewarm living. And that was what much of my Christian life was like.

The taproot of these weeds of failing to live by the Grace Priority and think from the Grace Perspective is the failure to realize that living and thinking this way is a choice – a Grace Preference – that must be made again and again, from the rooster's reveille to the Sandman's evening curtain. It was my failure to choose to live this way that kept me from experiencing God and the good He has the will and skill to do for me every day, all day long. I lived as a spiritual pauper even though I was a spiritual millionaire. Like an inheritance an heir doesn't even know is his, I left unclaimed much of the joy, peace, power, and contentment that were mine in my Lord's grace.

Had you eavesdropped on me, you'd have been as shocked at what I didn't and did say to myself as you'd be if I had cursed. I didn't constantly remind myself of who God is to me in Christ and what I am in the Savior. I habitually thought and talked as if grace had no more relevance to me than Julius Caesar. Doctrinally I affirmed grace; practically I denied it. I spoke of myself as if I were still in Adam, dead in trespasses and sins. I acted as if my daily sins made me *persona non grata* at the throne of grace, as if the thick curtain keeping me from the holy of holies was still there. I looked at trouble as if it were something the Lord sent

---

4. Genesis 42:36 (KJV).

to harm not help me, acting as if the Great Physician uses His scalpel on His children to scar not beautify us. The one note that was absent was the grace note of optimism. I wasn't regularly reminding myself that through Christ I can be sure I am God's child and my Father is *for* me, working all things for my good; and *with* me, helping me handle for His glory and my good whatever comes my way big and small.

If it were only myself I'd hurt by not living by the Grace Paradigm that would have been bad enough. But I wounded my brothers and sisters in Christ, too. Paul tells us, 'Bad company ruins good morals.'[5] Believers yoked to grace-minimizers at home or church or work know what he means. One grace-minimizing woman gave Job fits; ten grace-minimizing men severely damaged Israel; and nine grace-minimizing recipients of miraculous healing pained Jesus' heart.[6] Grace-minimizers are bad news. I have no doubt I was this kind of bad news to many on numerous occasions.

Were it not for God shifting my paradigm, I'd still be living this bankrupting life of grace-minimizing. Like a vagrant passing by a fine restaurant with an empty stomach, I'd still pass by moment by moment, situation by situation, need by need, duty by duty, and opportunity by opportunity without using grace to seize them for good. I'd still be living without much of the rhapsody and wonder of Christian living. But, bless His Name, God has shifted my paradigm.

I tell you this for two reasons. First, to glorify God for making me a Grace-Focused Optimist. I'm still just an

---

5. 1 Corinthians 15:33.

6. Job 2:9; Numbers 13 & 14; Luke 17:11-19.

apprentice in grace-governed living. But the apprenticeship is far better than the life I lived before God changed me. I give Him glory for giving such grace to me.

Second, I write to help my brothers and sisters in Christ. Years ago I heard a minister say, 'God will give *to* you what God can give *through* you.' I believe God has given me the truth of Grace-Focused Optimism because He wants to give it through me to others. So, if you're emotionally fragile; if breaking, pouting, moping, and discouragement characterize you far too often; if you're experiencing few of the grace pleasures available to you through Jesus and fear that you're not helping your brothers and sisters experience them either; or, if you're simply a believer in need of a fresh look at grace; I say to you that I believe God in His providence has brought Grace-Focused Optimism your way because He wants to help you shift to the Grace Paradigm.

God will shift your paradigm through the truths you'll find in the following chapters. The first of these truths is the Grace Priority. We turn to it now.

2

The Grace Priority
Grace Fact *One*: Committing to Grace-Governed Living

'In the New Testament, "grace" is a word of central importance – the keyword, in fact, of Christianity. Grace is what the New Testament is about ... Grace was to the Apostles the fundamental fact of life.'[1]

J. I. Packer

NUF SED

He called his bar the 'Third Base Saloon.' He said it was for regulars what third base was for baseball players: the last stop on the way home. His name was Michael T. McGreevey. But no one called him Michael or even Mike. Everyone called him 'Nuf Sed.' Why? Because he was the Mt. Sinai for the early 1900s Boston Red Sox. The final

---

1. J. I. Packer, *God's Words* (Downers Grove, Illinois: InterVarsity Press, 1981), p. 94.

word. When McGreevey spoke 'Nuf Sed.' The discussion was over.

God wants grace to be your 'Nuf Sed. *He wants you to commit to grace-governed living.* By 'commit to grace-governed living,' I mean God wants you to live and move and have your being in grace. He wants grace to be your hope and help, your courage and consolation, your motive and means, your dependence and delight, your habitat and happiness, and your prize and priority. He wants grace to define you. He wants you to think as a grace person, speak as a grace person, obey as a grace person, trust as a grace person, worship as a grace person, endure as a grace person, and love as a grace person. Committing to grace-governed living is the first step in changing to the Grace Paradigm.

I offer you seven biblical arguments that God wants you to commit to grace-governed living:

1. The first biblical argument that God wants you to commit to grace-governed living is the fact *He gives grace priority in His dealings with you.* A skillful maestro charms every musician into using his instrument to contribute to a standing ovation rendition of a symphony. The strings, woodwinds, brass, and percussions blend together to breathe auditory life into the composer's notes. God does something similar with you. He orchestrates every trait in His being so that it contributes to playing the grace symphony He wants your life to be. He commits all that He is to making you all He wants you to be.[2] Nothing less than

---

2. The assertions in this paragraph form the substance of this book. They'll be discussed in greater detail in the chapters that follow. Charles H. Spurgeon understands the point as well as anyone and expresses it better than everyone. Commenting on God's promise to Jacob in Genesis 32:12, he writes: "I will surely do thee good' is just the essence of the Lord's *gracious* sayings. Lay a

this is the meaning of, 'If God is for us who can be against us?'[3] God for you means all that God is – the totality of what makes Him God and not something else – is for you. His wisdom is for you. His faithfulness is for you. His mercy is for you. Even His justice is for you.[4] His providence toward you is grace providence.[5] His providing your needs is grace provision.[6] Your delights are grace pleasures.[7] Your pains are grace pains.[8] Grace is God's priority in all His dealings with you. If it's His priority, surely it ought to be yours.

2. The second biblical argument that God wants you to commit to grace-governed living is the fact *Jesus' glory is His grace*. We love asking someone intimate with a famous person, 'What's he like?' The apostles were Jesus' intimates. They lived with Him in the close-quartered situation foxhole-soldiers share. Like Noah with his pairs, Jesus dealt with all the animals in the human menagerie: from conniving kings to humiliated failures to arrogant hypocrites to disappointing disciples: proud people, weak

---

special stress on the word 'surely'. He will do us good, real good, lasting good, only good, every good. He will make us good, and this is to do us good in the very highest degree. He will treat us as he does his saints while we are here, and that is good. He will soon take us to be with Jesus and all his chosen, and this is supremely good. With this promise in our hearts we need not fear ... If the Lord will do us good, who can do us hurt?' Emphasis added. C. H. Spurgeon, *Cheque Book of the Bank of Faith*, (Scotland: Christian Focus Publications, 1996), p. 149. I believe Spurgeon's words are an excellent commentary on Romans 8:31 as well as Genesis 32:9.

3. Romans 8:31.

4. Romans 3:26; 1 John 1:9.

5. Hebrews 12:4-5; Romans 8:28.

6. 2 Corinthians 12:9; Hebrews 4:15-16.

7. 2 Corinthians 8:9; Psalm 23.

8. 2 Corinthians 12:7; Hebrews 12:5-11.

people, grieving people, duplicitous people, struggling people. Jesus' disciples saw Him rub shoulders with them all. Ask them, 'What was Jesus really like?' John answers for them: 'And the Word became flesh and dwelt among us, and we have seen his glory, glory as of the only Son from the Father, full of grace and truth ... And from his fullness we have all received, grace upon grace.'[9] To these men Jesus' grace stood out like a halo around a saint's head. Not His anger in the temple; not His fearlessness before the Pharisees; not His power to perform miracles, but His *grace* impressed them the most. He was the friend of sinners. He wouldn't break a bruised reed or quench a smoldering wick or give up on cowardly disciples. He even asked His Father to forgive the people who saw His death as good riddance.[10] At the heart of who Jesus is and what Jesus came to do is grace. Grace was His priority. If grace is Jesus' priority, shouldn't it be yours?

3. The third biblical argument that God wants you to commit to grace-governed living is the fact *the fundamental description of what it means for you to be a Christian is, 'You are not under law but under grace.'*[11] Being under grace means grace defines you. It means every line in your story is a

---

9. John 1:14, 16.

10. Matthew 11:19; Matthew 12:20; Luke 23:34.

11. Romans 6:14-15. The ESV Study Bible's comment on this verse makes the point: '... under grace means living under the new covenant in Christ, in an era characterized by grace.' *ESV Study Bible* (Wheaton, Illinois: Crossway Bibles, 2008), p. 2167. J. I. Packer writes, 'To live "not under law but under grace" (Romans 6:14f.), *in the sense of having one's whole relationship with God determined by His electing, redeeming, converting and protecting love, is the Christian's supreme privilege.' God's Words*, p. 106. Emphasis added. Note that Packer defines 'under grace' as being governed by grace (= having one's whole relationship with God determined by his ... love).

grace line. The plot is a grace plot. Every character is a grace character. Every chapter is a grace chapter. Every paragraph is a grace paragraph. Every sentence is a grace sentence. The dialogue is grace dialogue. The climax is a grace climax. The conclusion will be a grace conclusion. And the author of the whole is a grace Author. 'Twas grace hath made your heart to fear and grace your fears relieved. 'Twas grace that brought you safe thus far, 'tis grace shall lead you home.'[12] You are inexplicable without grace. Grace is your DNA. God never thinks of you as anything other than a grace person. He never addresses you as anything other than a grace person. He never deals with you as anything other than a grace person. Surely if this is the way God thinks of you it's the way you ought to think of yourself.[13]

4. The fourth biblical argument that God wants you to commit to grace-governed living is the fact *the help He gives you is grace help*. Like me, you live a 9-1-1 life. We share a constant need for God's help. Praise His name, He delights in helping. Luther is right in describing the Lord as 'Our Helper he amid the flood of mortal ills prevailing.' And the help He delights in giving is grace help. Take a few for instances. When you pray you draw near to a 'throne of grace.' There you 'receive mercy and find grace to help

---

12. John Newton, 'Amazing Grace', stanzas 2 and 3 paraphrased.

13. We are *elected* by grace, Ephesians 1:4. We are *saved* by grace, Ephesians 2:8-9. We are *called* by grace, Galatians 1:6. We are *justified* by grace, Romans 3:24. We are *forgiven* by grace, Ephesians 2:5. *Jesus' saving career* culminating in His cross and resurrection is God's abounding grace, Romans 5:20. The *secure position* we have in Christ is standing in grace, Romans 5:2. Witnessing a great number of people believing and turning to the Lord is called *seeing* the grace of God, Acts 11:23. Christians' *gifts* are grace gifts, Romans 12:6, Ephesians 4:7. The *coming life of perfection* is described as grace, 1 Peter 1:3. Surely this is 'Nuf Sed!'

in time of need.'[14] Trials come. One thing can help you handle them like Job instead of like Job's wife. That one thing is what helped Paul handle the thorn Jesus wouldn't pull out: 'My grace is sufficient for you, for my power is made perfect in weakness.'[15] Your weakness is the venue for His strength. His strength is described as His sufficient grace. Again, you turn to God's Word because you believe Jesus when he tells you, 'Man shall not live by bread alone, but by every word that comes from the mouth of God.'[16] This word can make you wiser than Solomon. This word can make you stronger than Samson. This word can make you a tree planted by streams of water, yielding its fruit in season. This word is the sword of the Spirit by which you can imitate your Savior and slash Satan to ribbons with 'It is written. It is written. It is written.' And one word sums up this Word: grace. The Bible is 'the word of His grace, which is able to build you up and to give you the inheritance among all those who are sanctified.'[17] You can't live without God's help. God's help is grace help. Surely grace ought to have priority in your life.

5. The fifth biblical argument that God wants you to commit to grace-governed living is the fact *the hope He gives you is grace hope.* Living for the Lord is like training for the Olympics. Follow an Olympic athlete. She goes through a grueling regime in prepping for the games. She sacrifices pleasures others enjoy. Everything from friendship to McDonald's fries takes a back seat to her practice. What

---

14. Hebrews 4:16.

15. 2 Corinthians 12:9.

16. Matthew 4:4.

17. Acts 20:32.

keeps her going? The possibility of standing on the center podium—gold medal draping her chest, sensory neurons causing goose bump pride—as her country's flag is raised and its national anthem played. You call this prospect of future good 'hope.' It's the same for you. You say with Peter, 'Lord, we have left everything and followed you.'[18] You take up your cross daily and walk the *Via Dolorosa*; you pluck out eyes, you cut off hands; you flee youthful lusts warring against your soul; you lay up treasures in heaven; as much as it depends on you, you live peaceably with everyone; you don't avenge yourself but leave vengeance to the Lord; you bless those who curse you; you forgive those who wrong you; you walk in love as Christ loved you.[19] Truth be told, all this makes the Olympian grind seem like a week in Acapulco. What keeps you going? The certainty something infinitely better than a gold medal awaits you. What? That 'in the coming ages' God will 'show the immeasurable riches of His grace in kindness toward you in Christ Jesus.'[20] The central incentive for living a Christian life is the certainty that 'grace will be brought to you at the revelation of Jesus Christ.'[21] If grace is the priority for your future, shouldn't it be your priority in the present?

6. The sixth biblical argument that God wants you to commit to grace-governed living is the fact that *the sole way God aims to get glory from you is by giving grace to you.* The divine potter has made you a vessel of mercy prepared

18. Mark 10:28.

19. Luke 9:23; Matthew 5:29-30; 2 Timothy 2:22; Matthew 6:19-21; Romans 12:18-21; Ephesians 4:31-5:2.

20. Ephesians 2:7.

21. 1 Peter 1:13.

for glory.[22] He is out to make you like Jesus not Pharaoh. You are a Jacob not an Esau; a Sarah not a Jezebel. You aren't this because you're better than Pharaoh or Jezebel. You're 'of the same lump'[23] as they. You're different because God is out to cause you to glory in His goodness, revel in His redemption, delight in His deliverance, and savor His sovereignty. In other words, God is out to make you 'praise the glory of his grace.'[24] If God makes grace His priority for getting glory from you, shouldn't grace be your priority?

7. The seventh biblical argument that God wants you to commit to grace-governed living is the fact *the final statement the Bible makes is a grace statement.* Imagine you're on your deathbed. Your family is gathered around. The spouse who helped make your life a good life is on one side holding your hand. The children you love with all your heart are on the other side. They're gently stroking your head, tenderly caressing your hand, telling you how much they love you. You know you're dying. They know you're dying. You have breath enough to gasp out one final statement. What will you say? Surely your final word will be significant. Surely you'll stress what's most important to you. Last words matter: with us; with God. Here's God's last word to you: 'The grace of our Lord Jesus Christ be with all. Amen.'[25] Of all the things God could have said to you—of all the exhortations, all the

---

22. Romans 9:23.

23. Romans 9:21.

24. Romans 9:6-23; Ephesians 1:6, 12, 14.

25. Revelation 22:21.

promises, all the warnings He could have chosen—with an unlimited imagination and an infinite vocabulary at His disposal; a burning love and tender concern for you in His heart—with all of this, His last word is a grace word! He gives priority to grace in the final sentence He speaks to you! Doesn't this demand that you give grace priority in your life?

Here are seven evidences that God's thoughts become your thoughts and God's ways become your ways when His grace governs your life. When you begin giving grace priority by allowing it to govern your life, you take the first step in shifting to the Grace Paradigm.

Go ahead and take this step now. After all, God wants YOU to commit to grace-governed living.

'Nuf Sed.

3

The Grace Perspective
Grace Fact *Two*: Understanding that Faith is Optimism about God

'If you take the biblical view of history you can put it like this: *in the immediate it is pessimistic.* But, thank God, that is only in the immediate. *In the ultimate it is optimistic.* The Bible pours scorn and ridicule upon the various movements of idealism in human history, for they never come to anything. Civilizations rise and wane. The world seems to be reaching what seems to be perfection and then it crashes down. In 1914 all seemed to be going well; then came the crash. It has always been like that. *In the immediate the Bible is always pessimistic.* You read about the opening of the seals and the pouring out of the vials and everything seems to be against the elect; there is immediate suffering, apparent defeat. *But it is only in the immediate. The ultimate is always optimistic, for always at the end we are reminded of the power of Christ.* At the end we see everything that has raised its arrogant head against the Lord of glory defeated and cast into the lake of fire, utterly

destroyed. *God and his saints triumph over all and there is a new heaven and a new earth, and the glory of God is revealed.'*
Dr. D. Martyn Lloyd-Jones.[1]

'The Pessimist is not a representative of Christianity.'
A. T. Robertson[2]

THEY ALL CARRY A 15ᵀᴴ CLUB IN THEIR BAGS

The rules of golf permit a golfer to carry fourteen clubs in his bag. But golf psychologist Bob Rotella says every great golfer carries a 15th club. That 15th club is confidence. Great golfers are confident about their skills.[3] The Bible declares that grace people all carry a 15th club in their bags, too. It's not the club of confidence in themselves. It's the club of confidence in God. And confidence in God is optimism about him. Optimism about God is the Grace Perspective. The Grace Perspective is Grace Fact 2: *God wants you to live every day, all day long, with the attitude of optimism about Him.*

'Optimism' isn't a word usually associated with Christianity. If you were doing a crossword puzzle and fifteen down read 'an eight letter word for the Christian attitude toward life' you probably wouldn't put o-p-t-i-m-i-s-m in the squares. So, allow me to tell you what I do and do not mean by this word.

---

1. David Martyn Lloyd-Jones, *The Christian in an Age of Terror* (Grand Rapids: Kregel Publications, 2008), p. 202. Emphasis added.

2. John Blanchard, *Sifted Silver* (England: Evangelical Press, 1995), p. 31.

3. Dr. Bob Rotella, *Your 15ᵗʰ Club: The Inner Secret to Great Golf,* (New York: Free Press, 2008), p. 14.

1. What This Optimism Is Not

The optimism God wants you to have isn't *temperamental*. You may be congenitally pessimistic, the genetic Siamese twin of Charlie Brown in biological wiring. It doesn't matter. You can be an optimist in the sense God wants no matter what your temperament.

The optimism God wants you to have isn't *circumstantial*. Its habitat isn't sunshine. It can survive and thrive in winter bleakness and summer heat. The coldest temperatures won't freeze its vines. The longest drought won't dry its stalks and spoil its crop. You can be an optimist in the sense God wants no matter what your circumstances.

The optimism God wants you to have isn't *nonsensical*. It's not Dr. Seuss unrealistic. It's not naïve. It's not absurd. It's not myopic. It looks with 20/20 clarity at sin, sorrow, savagery, and everything else scarring this East of Eden world. Yet nothing jades it; nothing sours it; nothing douses it. Just the opposite: its flag unfurls to its fullest when reality's rude winds blow the hardest. You can be an optimist in the sense God wants even when life puzzles and perplexes you.

The optimism God wants you to have isn't *emotional*. It isn't a feeling. It isn't a mood that comes and goes like a tide. This optimism has more to do with your thinking and willing than it does with your sensations. So, it can live with the worst of feelings, as a godly woman can live with a less than godly husband. And it can tame emotions and bring them under control so that the inmates don't run the asylum. You can be an optimist in the sense God wants even when you're feeling bad physically or emotionally.

2. What This Optimism Is

What is this optimism that isn't temperamental, circum-stantial, nonsensical, or emotional? It's *theological* optimism. It's optimism about God. This makes it realistic optimism. God is I AM. He is ultimate reality. It's *doctrinal* optimism. It lives and moves and has its being in the biblical truth that grace means God is determined to do you good and His determination governs all of His dealings with you. It's *practical* optimism. It helps you live a God-glorifying, God-enjoying life as nothing else can. It's *doxological* optimism. It gives you a thousand tongues to sing your great Redeemer's praise. And, because of these things, it's *essential* optimism. You need it to be the Christian God wants you to be.

This optimism that's theological, doctrinal, practical, doxological, and essential is the Grace Perspective. The Grace Perspective teaches you that grace gives you reason to be optimistic about God from sunup to sundown. Living by the Grace Perspective is the heart of grace-governed living. When you live every day, all day long, with an attitude of optimism about God, you are living a grace-governed life.

I offer you the following confirmation that living a grace-governed life means living with an attitude of optimism toward God: *The Bible demonstrates that Grace People live by faith and the heart of faith is optimism about God.*

I. *The Bible demonstrates that grace people live by faith.* Grace people glory in the grace priority. They relish the fact God wants them to live grace-governed lives. They need grace more than a newborn needs the care of its mother; they want grace more than that newborn craves its mother's milk. That's why faith is so important to them. They know the way to experience God's grace is through faith. That's how their grace-governed life began: 'For by grace you have been saved through faith.'[4] That's how their grace-governed life continues. Grace people are 'the just who live by faith.'[5] They live by faith in the sense of *eternal life* and in the sense of *everyday living*. Grace people are people who live in moment-by- moment faith dependence on the grace of God, turning to Him for His help every day, all day long.

II. *Jesus says the heart of faith is optimism about God.* He says this in Matthew 8:5-13.[6] The passage tells a familiar story. A centurion[7] has a servant who is one-foot-in-the-grave sick. The doctor's grim prescription is 'Let's make his last few hours as comfortable as possible.' But the soldier refuses to wave a white flag. He comes to Jesus and says: 'Lord, at your say-so my servant's illness will vanish; he'll

---

4. Ephesians 2:8.

5. Romans 1:17 and Galatians 2:20-21 characterize the entire Christian life as a life of depending on grace through faith. Again, Romans 15:13, for example, teaches that the grace gifts of 'joy and peace' come to us through 'believing.'

6. 'When he had entered Capernaum, a centurion came forward to him, appealing to him, 'Lord, my servant is lying paralyzed at home, suffering terribly.' And he said to him, "I will come and heal him." But the centurion replied, "Lord, I am not worthy to have you come under my roof, but only say the word, and my servant will be healed. For I too am a man under authority, with soldiers under me. And I say to one, 'Go,' and he goes, and to another, 'Come,' and he comes, and to my servant, 'Do this,' and he does it." When Jesus heard this, he marveled and said to those who followed him, "Truly, I tell you, with no one in Israel have I found such faith. I tell you, many will come from east and west and recline at table with Abraham, Isaac, and Jacob in the kingdom of heaven, while the sons of the kingdom will be thrown into the outer darkness. In that place there will be weeping and gnashing of teeth." And to the centurion Jesus said, "Go; let it be done for you as you have believed." And the servant was healed at that very moment.'

7. 'The *centurion* and his *servant* were non-Jewish soldiers in the army of occupation.' *New Bible Commentary*, (Downers Grove, Illinois: Inter-Varsity Press, 1953), p. 915. Italics in original.

pull out his tubes, get up, take off that silly hospital gown, put on his clothes and walk out of ICU fit as a fiddle. He won't need rehab or have to take it easy for a while. I know you can cause this to happen.'

I don't know what you call this if you don't call it *optimism* about Jesus.[8] Missionary William Carey's motto was, 'Expect great things of God; attempt great things for God.' This officer expects great things of Jesus. We say of a tough task, 'It's easier said than done.' This man gives Jesus the toughest of tasks and says, 'Lord, it's done as easy as you saying it.' He's confident – optimistic – the Lord can do what he asks.

Notice what Jesus calls this man's optimism: 'faith.' Jesus gives faith top billing on this incident's silver screen. In fact, Jesus says when you look at him you're looking at an Academy Award winning performance. He awards the centurion's faith the Oscar of 'marveling' at it: 'When Jesus heard this, he marveled and said to those who followed him, "Truly, I tell you, with no one in Israel have I found such faith."' Sit in the dark theater of this man's trouble and you see a full-length feature of believing in action. And that believing is optimism about Jesus. You live a grace-governed life by living a life of faith; and you live a life of faith by being optimistic about God. This is what makes you a grace person.

III. Maybe you're thinking I've overplayed my hand. After all, the story of the centurion is just one story.

---

8. Please remember that Jesus is God (John 14:9): therefore, faith in Him is faith in God; optimism about Him is optimism about His Father.

Is it right to generalize from it that the heart of faith is optimism about God? Maybe it would be if his story were the only card I hold. It isn't. I've got a deck full of others. Again and again, the Bible demonstrates that grace people are people characterized by optimism about God and His Son and that this optimism *is* faith. I offer you now five more examples of the truth that faith is optimism about God.

1. *Abraham* is my flagship example. Remember his importance. He is supremely, Jesus excepted, 'the man of faith.'[9] When you look at him you look at the God-authorized model of what it means for you to live by faith. What does Abraham show you about faith? Listen to the answer given by the best alumnus of Abraham's school: 'In hope he believed against hope, that he should become the father of many nations, as he had been told, "So shall your offspring be." He did not weaken in faith when he considered his own body, which was as good as dead (since he was about a hundred years old), or when he considered the barrenness of Sarah's womb. No unbelief made him waver concerning the promise of God, but he grew strong in his faith as he gave glory to God, fully convinced that God was able to do what he had promised.'[10]

Consider Abraham's rock and hard place situation: his age puts him past the medically miraculous help of Viagra. Sarah's ancient womb isn't child friendly either. Humanly speaking, neither has any more ability to produce a child

9. Galatians 3:9.
10. Romans 4:18-21.

than a plastic plant has of growing leaves. But we're not humanly speaking here. We're *divinely* speaking. God has made Abraham a stork promise. 'I'm going to give you and Sarah a son.' Then God does what he often does: He takes His time in keeping His promise. A lot of time. Abraham waits. And waits. And waits. What keeps him going? He is optimistic God won't let him down: He is 'fully convinced that God was able to do what He had promised.' Abraham is a grace person. This means he believes. And his believing is optimism about God.

2. *David* is my next example that faith is optimism about God. The Bible gives David this standing ovation testimony: He was 'a man after God's own heart.'[11] That means he was a man who pleased God – not perfectly, but genuinely. And that means the chief characteristic of David's life was faith because 'without faith it is impossible to please God.'[12] You learn the core of this God-prized man's faith when you listen to him volunteer for the seemingly suicidal mission of fighting Goliath. You know the story. David tells Saul he'll fight the Philistine bully. Saul's hesitant to accept his offer. It's not good politics to send a boy home in a body bag. The king tries to shoo the shepherd away with demoralizing words. David won't listen. Why not? He has a history with God of beating the odds. He tells Saul of a time a starving bear came to dine on his flock. David killed the bear. Then there was the time a famished lion tried to put his sheep on its menu. David killed the lion. Now the

11. Acts 13:22.

12. Hebrews 11:6.

lion's head is on the wall, and the bear's skin is on the floor, in Jesse's den. David is sure this Philistine wolf will soon join them in taxidermy-produced perpetuity. How can he be so certain? Listen: 'The Lord who delivered me from the paw of the lion and the paw of the bear will deliver me from the hand of this Philistine.'[13] David is optimistic that God won't let him down. David is a grace person. This means he believes. And his believing is optimism about God.

3. Example three that faith is optimism about God is the witness of Israel's two Congressional Medal of Honor winners *Caleb* and *Joshua*. They're members of the elite twelve-man Army Ranger reconnaissance unit parachuting behind enemy lines. The men find everything there BIG: big grapes; big people; big problems. The big problems dwarf the little faith of ten of the spies. Their courage goes AWOL. When Moses debriefs them they tell him this is an impossible mission. Their contagious cowardice infects the people. God describes their majority report as unbelief.[14] This means what Caleb and Joshua do involves believing God. What do they do? They disagree with the other spies. They say the mission is possible. Listen to their spine-tingling call to arms: 'And Caleb stilled the people before Moses, and said, "Let us go up at once and possess it; for we are well able to overcome it."'[15] Where did Caleb get such confidence? Joshua tells you: 'Only do not rebel against the Lord, neither fear the people of the land, for they are

---

13. 1 Samuel 17:33-37.

14. Numbers 14:11.

15. Numbers 13:30 (KJV).

bread for us; their defense is departed from them and the Lord is with us: fear them not.'[16] What attitude are they expressing in the words, 'the Lord is with us'? Optimism. They're optimistic about God, confident He won't let them down. Caleb and Joshua are grace people. This means they believe. And their believing is optimism about God.

4. *Paul* next testifies that faith is optimism about God. His story is rousing. He is a passenger on an Italy-bound ship. But this is no pleasure cruise. He is in the custody of Roman FBI agents. They're escorting him to his Supreme Court rendezvous with Caesar. The ship runs into the perfect storm. The crew and passengers sense doom. Luke chills us with cold-to-the-bone bleakness by writing, 'And when neither sun nor stars in many days appeared, and no small tempest lay on us, all hope that we should be saved was then taken away.'[17] Then God sends a Coast Guard angel to tell Paul the boat will sink but the passengers will survive. Paul immediately passes on the good news: 'And now I exhort you to be of good cheer: for there shall be no loss of any man's life among you, but of the ship.'[18] Nothing has changed outwardly: the sun and stars still aren't shining; the tempest still rages. Yet smack dab in the middle of a storm Paul is optimistic about God, convinced He is going to keep His promise and save everyone on board. And he calls this optimism about the Lord – based solely on God's promise – *faith*! 'For this very night,' (he

---

16. Numbers 14:9 (KJV).

17. Acts 27:20 (KJV).

18. Acts 27:22 (KJV).

is giving his fellow passengers the Page 2 rest of the story explanation about why they should cheer up), 'there stood before me an angel of the God to whom I belong and whom I worship, and he said, "Do not be afraid, Paul; you must stand before Caesar. And behold, God has granted you all those who sail with you." So take heart, men, for *I have faith in God* that it will be exactly as I have been told.'[19] Paul is a grace person. This means he believes. And his believing is optimism about God.

5. I have saved for last the best example that faith is optimism about God: *Jesus*. He is preeminently *THE* man of faith. We don't usually think of our Lord this way. But the Bible does. Hebrews describes Jesus as 'the author and finisher of faith.'[20] English translations add 'our.' The addition subtracts because it draws attention from the point being made. That point isn't about our faith; it's about Jesus' faith.[21] Jesus is the supreme example of what it means to live by faith. The writer is saying, 'Do you want

---

19. Acts 27:23-25. Emphasis added. John Stott captures Paul's optimism: God's 'divine promises were the foundation of Paul's summons to everybody to maintain courage. For he believed in God, in his character and covenant, and was convinced that he would keep his promises …' John Stott, *The Spirit, The Church & The World*, (Downers Grove, Illinois: InterVarsity Press, 1990), p. 391.

20. Hebrews 12:2 (KJV).

21. 'In Hebrews 12:2 where Christ is called the 'Author and Perfecter of faith,' He is represented as the One who takes precedence in faith and is thus the perfect Exemplar of it. The pronoun 'our' does not correspond to anything in the original, and may well be omitted. Christ in the days of His flesh trod undeviatingly the path of faith, and as the Perfecter has brought it to a perfect end in His own Person. Thus He is the leader of all others who tread that path.' W. E. Vine, *An Expository Dictionary of New Testament Words* (Old Tappan, New Jersey: Fleming H. Revell Company, 1940), p. 88.

to know what it means to believe through thick and thin? Look at Jesus! There isn't a single flaw in His faith diamond. He showed no hospitality to doubt. He never cried, 'Lord, I believe, help my unbelief.' Jesus' life is a believing life from start to finish.'[22]

What does it mean for Jesus to believe? It means He is optimistic about God. Have you ever noticed as you read the Gospels that Jesus *almost never* talks about Good Friday without talking about Easter Sunday?[23] Why not? He is optimistic the grave won't have the final word. What makes Him optimistic? God's promise! You see this preeminently at Calvary. When Jesus is on the cross Psalm 22 is on His mind.[24] This Psalm

22. 'He trusts in God,' they said as they stood by his cross; the implication was: "Much good His trust in God is doing Him now!" The words, though not their implication, were truer than they knew. *The whole life of Jesus was characterized by unbroken and unquestioning faith in His heavenly Father.... It was sheer faith in God, unsupported by any visible or tangible evidence, that carried Him through the taunting, the scourging, the crucifying, and the more bitter agony of rejection, desertion and dereliction.' F. F. Bruce, *The New International Commentary on the New Testament: Hebrews* (Grand Rapids: Wm. B. Eerdmans Publishing Company, 1964), p. 352. The eloquent words of Hugh Martin echo Bruce's recognition of the supremacy of faith in Jesus: 'So eminent and obvious was the faith which Jesus reposed in God that it was a matter of reproach to him. "All they that see me laugh me to scorn: they shoot out the lip, they shake the head, saying, He trusted on the Lord that he would deliver him; let him deliver him seeing he delighted in him." Such was the prophetic testimony of the Spirit. And it was literally fulfilled: for "the chief priests mocking him, with the scribes and elders said, 'He trusted in God; let him deliver him now if he will have him' (Ps. 22:8; Matt. 27:43). His faith was conspicuous even to his foes."' Hugh Martin, *The Shadow of Calvary* (Edinburgh: The Banner of Truth Trust, 1983 reprint), p. 64.

23. See, for example, the following: Matthew 16:21; Mark 9:31; Mark 10:33-34; Luke 9:22; Luke 18:33; John 10:17-18.

24. 'In uttering this cry (i.e., the cry of dereliction, CLC), Jesus was using words taken from the Old Testament, in this case Psalm 22:1. It should not escape our attention that *often* during his earthly ministry Jesus *drew his strength from the Old Testament... .(E)ven during the final hours of his life on earth before he*

speaks of a man coping with a Good Friday sorrow through the assurance of an Easter Sunday triumph.[25] Jesus knows this psalm is talking about Him. He embraces it as His Father's promise to bring the great good of God-glorifying salvation out of His death. This is the 'joy set before him' by which he 'endured the cross.'[26] This is the core of His faith. In the midst of the blackness of judgment, Jesus is optimistic about God, optimistic that God is determined to bring Him from the tomb as Lord and Savior. When you look at Jesus, the Author and Perfecter of faith – in other words, the man, the *only* man, who perfectly lived out what it means to live by faith – you see that faith is optimism about God!

I trust this chapter shows you that faith is optimism about God. Understand this, and you understand living by faith. You're living by faith when you live with optimism about God. When you begin living with optimism about God you begin living with the Grace Perspective. When

---

died, Jesus made use of passages from the sacred writings again and again.' William Hendrickson, *New Testament Commentary: Mark* (Grand Rapids: Baker Book House, 1975), p. 66. Emphasis added.

25. Leland Ryken & Philip Graham Ryken, *The Literary Study Bible* (Wheaton, Illinois: Good News Publishers, 2007), p. 766, have this note: 'This poem is a memorable expression of the suffering soul. The poem speaks in universal terms that all people in distress can echo as expressing their feelings. But this is also a poem of "second meanings" in which many of the sentiments were preeminently true of the Messiah in the sacrificial sufferings of his passion and death (see, for example, Matt. 27:46). The sequence of feelings is as follows: opening cry of distress to God (vv. 1-2); foil – God's deliverance of his people in the past (vv. 3-5); return to the present: the speaker's extreme suffering and rejection (vv. 6-18); petition that God deliver the speaker (vv. 19-21a); praise of God for his deliverance (vv. 21b-31). It is evident that while the first half of the poem belongs to the lament psalm, the conventions of the praise psalm dominate the second half.'

26. Hebrews 12:2.

you begin living with the Grace Perspective you begin living the Grace-governed life God wants you to live.

Isn't it time for you to begin carrying a 15th club in your bag?

4

The Grace Preference
Grace Fact *Three*: Choosing to Be Optimistic About God

'The longer I live, the more I realize the impact of attitude on life. Attitude, to me, is more important than facts. It is more important than the past, than education, than money, than circumstances, than failures, than successes, than what other people think or say or do. It is more important than appearance, giftedness or skill. It will make or break a company … a church … a home. *The remarkable thing is we have a choice every day regarding the attitude we will embrace for that day.* We cannot change our past … we cannot change the fact that people will act in a certain way. We cannot change the inevitable. The only thing we can do is play on the one string we have, and that is our attitude … I am convinced that life is 10 per cent what happens to me and 90 per cent how I react to it. And so it is with you … *we are in charge of our attitudes.'*

Chuck Swindoll[1]

---

1. http://faculty.klutztown.edu/friehauf/attitude.html (Emphasis added).

CHARLIE RUGG'S MANTRA

Long ago, in a galaxy far, far away, I played college basketball at Belhaven College in Jackson, Mississippi. Charlie Rugg was my coach. Coach was known for his Mt. Vesuvius temper. Bobby Knight had nothing on him. Sometimes Charlie was a better show than his team. When a ref's call displeased him, he'd engage in assault and battery on a chair by kicking it. Every now and then, he'd get so enraged he'd pull off his sport coat as if it were on fire and toss it away. Technical fouls were on a first name basis with Coach. Then something wonderful happened. The storm maker met the storm breaker. Charlie became a Christian. Old things passed away; all things became new. Nothing was newer about Coach than his on-court demeanor. One night after his conversion a bad call was made. A really bad call, the kind that would have tempted even Billy Graham to kick a chair were he coaching. Team statistician Orly Hood, nervous as a dog eyeing its abusive owner, peeked at Charlie. Nothing moved but Coach's lips. Orly leaned closer to hear what The Man was saying to himself. Here's what he heard: 'To act like a Christian, I've got to think like a Christian. To act like a Christian, I've got to think like a Christian.' Coach's mantra was spot on. Grace living depends on grace thinking.

Grace thinking involves making the Grace Preference. The Grace Preference is the choice to have an attitude of optimism about God. Here's the proposition: *God wants you to CHOOSE to be optimistic about Him every day, all day long by choosing to focus on grace exclusively and continuously.*

I. Optimism about God is a *choice* you make. Remember, optimism about Him is the essence of faith. And God wants you to believe. 'Have faith in God'[2] is Jesus' one sentence summary of God's desire for you. Practically speaking, this means 'Be optimistic about God' every day, all day long. This optimism isn't a fire lit by a lightning strike. It won't just happen. It's a fireplace fire. You must choose to build it. If the fire of optimism about God is burning in you at any given moment it's because you decided to take dry, seasoned grace kindling and logs and light them. If it continues burning it's because you choose to tend it, stoke it, and add grace wood to it again and again. God wants you to choose to light the optimism fire and keep it blazing every day all day long.

II. You choose to be optimistic about God by choosing to *focus* on grace. Something that happened to Baptist pastor Charles Stanley illustrates the importance of focus. He was once the rope in a factional tug-of-war in his church. One faction was thumbs up, the other thumbs down. You can imagine Stanley's stress level. After a while an elderly lady in the congregation became his Good Samaritan. She invited Stanley to her house. During the visit she showed him a picture on her wall. Stanley looked up at a magnificent portrayal of Daniel in the lion's den. The sister asked her pastor to describe the picture. Stanley mentioned the lions' closed mouths and Daniel's calmness. Then this godly woman put her arm around her pastor's shoulders and preached what he called one of the greatest sermons he'd ever heard. 'Son,' she said, 'what I want you to see is, Daniel doesn't have his eyes on the lions but on the

2. Mark 11:22.

Lord.'[3] That's focus. Focus is putting all your attention on something and keeping it there. If you're going to choose the Grace Preference of living with optimism about God you must focus on grace. Only grace can keep you optimistic about God every day, all day long. And grace will only do this as you focus on it. So, you must choose to put all your attention on grace and keep it there. You must choose to be preoccupied with grace. You must choose to be obsessed with grace. You must choose to be mesmerized by grace.

III. You choose to focus on grace by *learning everything you can about what grace means for you individually.* Paul tells you what God does for you 'to the praise of his glorious grace' in Ephesians 1:3-14. He then prays, 'that the God of our Lord Jesus Christ, the Father of glory, may give you a spirit of wisdom and of revelation in the knowledge of him, having the eyes of your hearts enlightened, that you may know what is the hope to which he has called you, what are the riches of his glorious inheritance in the saints, and what is the immeasurable greatness of his power toward us who believe, according to the working of his great might that he worked in Christ when he raised him from the dead and seated him at his right hand in the heavenly places, far above all rule and authority and power and dominion, and above every name that is named not only in this age but also in the age to come. And he put all things under his feet and gave him as head over all things to the church, which is his body, the fullness of him who fills all in all.'[4] You

---

3. http://www.intouch.org/magazine/content/topic/our_prince_of_peace
4. Ephesians 1:17-23.

can summarize this prayer in one sentence: 'Father, allow your children to know what your grace means to them individually!' Christian, MAKE THIS YOUR DESIRE! Refuse to rest in kindergarten thoughts about grace. Don't be content with knowing grace's ABC's. And don't stop with a high school diploma in grace either. Choose to go after a grace PhD. Choose to become an expert in grace by learning everything you can about what grace means for you individually.

IV. You choose to learn all you can about grace by *choosing to embrace God's grace talk to you in the Bible.* Your Bible is God's grace talk to you. It's 'the word of his grace.'[5] God's grace talk reveals His grace attitude and intentions toward you. He isn't shy about His grace. He wears His grace thoughts about you on His sleeve and shouts His grace ways with you from the rooftops. He does this throughout the Bible, especially in the New Testament. When you read it you learn what grace is for you individually. You learn that grace is God's always-positive attitude toward you and always-constructive activity with you. It's His heart and His hand demonstrated in all that He has done, is doing, and will do for you through Jesus and by the Holy Spirit. It's His love for you and His loyalty to you. It's His plan, providence, and provision dedicated to making you permanently and perfectly happy by making you permanently and perfectly like Jesus. Believer, God has gone out of His way to speak His grace things to you. Choose to embrace them! Don't be wayside soil with these precious grace facts. Don't think they can't possibly belong

---

5. Acts 20:32.

to you. Receive them as you would a fabulous inheritance bequeathed to you by a rich aunt who doted on you! Receive them this way because they ARE a fabulous inheritance bequeathed to *you* by your gracious God. As a believer in Jesus, all grace's treasures and pleasures are yours. As a believer in Jesus, all grace's gifts and goodness are yours. As a believer in Jesus, all grace's sweetness and splendor are yours. Listen to God speaking to you through Paul: 'All things are yours.'[6] Elect woman, man in Christ, *choose* to embrace this. *Choose* to believe it. *Choose* to take at face value what God says about you in grace! *Choose* to do this and you stack grace wood you can use to light the fire of optimism about God and keep it blazing every day, all day long.

V. The way you take the wood from the cord and use it to build the fire of optimism about God and keep it going is by *choosing to focus on grace in your thinking and self-talk every day, all day long.* You must choose to focus on grace in your *thinking.* Can you choose your thoughts? Yes! You can choose to swat away graceless thoughts as you swat away mosquitoes on a hot summer evening. And you can choose to focus on grace thoughts as a bride and groom focus on the preacher's words in their wedding ceremony. Paul makes that clear when he commands you 'Finally, brothers, whatever is true, whatever is honorable, whatever is just, whatever is pure, whatever is lovely, whatever is commendable, if there is any excellence, if there is anything worthy of praise, think about these things.'[7] Hummingbird

---

6. 1 Corinthians 3:22.

7. Philippians 4:8. J. I. Packer comments on this verse, 'Can we really choose what we are going to think about? In these days, when we are endlessly overstimulated from outside and the ever-present TV encourages the passive

thoughts flit through your mind all day. But they don't stay unless you build them birdhouses! You choose the thoughts you show hospitality to. God wants you to choose to be hospitable to grace thoughts alone and rude to every other kind of thinking. Making grace thoughts feel welcome is a habit you can develop.

Along with focusing on grace in your thinking, you've got to focus on it in *your self-talk as well.* You may be quiet as stone around other people but there's one person you talk to constantly: you. And God wants you to choose to talk to yourself the way He talks to you. His way of talking to you is exclusively and continuously a grace way. He always speaks of you, and to you, as a grace person. You must choose to do the same until grace self-talk is your habit.

Paul is your model here. *Eavesdrop on the way he thinks about, and speaks to, himself.* You won't find anything but grace words, grace sentences, and grace paragraphs; and, grace labels, grace reminders, grace exhortations, and grace encouragements. He does this exclusively and continuously. He is 'a man in Christ.' He revels in the thought, 'Christ loved me and gave himself for me.' He defines himself and his achievements with the words, 'By the grace of God I am what I am.' Even when he calls himself the 'chief of sinners' it's in a grace magnifying context focusing on 'the grace of our Lord Jesus Christ' and beginning with 'I thank him who has given me strength, Christ Jesus our Lord' and

---

mind-set that makes us wait to be entertained, the idea of regularly choosing themes for our thoughts seems strange to the point of freakiness. But Paul has no doubt that thought-control of this kind is possible. He actually commands it.' *Hot Tub Religion* (Wheaton, Illinois: Tyndale Publishing House, 1988), pp. 157-158.

ending with 'To the King of the ages, immortal, invisible, the only God, be honor and glory forever and ever. Amen'.[8]

Paul does the same with believers. He engages in grace talk with Christians even when they're sheep who aren't following the Shepherd's voice. Look at Corinth. Talk about a black sheep congregation. Those Christians were struggling with core doctrines like the resurrection and were tolerating shameful sexual sin. You'd think Paul would address them with Drill Sergeant severe words. He does just the opposite. 'Paul ... to the church of God that is in Corinth, to those sanctified in Christ Jesus, called to be saints ... Grace to you and peace from God our Father and the Lord Jesus Christ.'[9] What's going on? Paul's modeling the way you should think about yourself and speak to yourself. And that's the way of grace. That's the *only* way you're to think and speak. And you're to choose to think and speak this way *all the time.*

When you choose to think and speak as a grace person, you choose to focus on grace. When you choose to focus on grace you make the Grace Preference. When the Grace Preference becomes your daily way of living, you take the third step in shifting to the Grace Paradigm.

Go ahead and take that step now.

Take it because Charlie Rugg is right.

To act like a Christian you've got to think like a Christian.

---

8. 1 Timothy 1:12-17.

9. 1 Corinthians 1:1-3.

5

Grace Pleasures
Grace Fact *Four*: Enjoying Grace Every Day, All Day Long

'"I will surely do thee good" is just the essence of all the Lord's gracious sayings. Lay a special stress on the word "surely." He will do us good, real good, lasting good, only good, every good. He will make us good, and this is to do us good in the very highest degree. He will treat us as he does his saints while we are here, and that is good. He will soon take us to be with Jesus and all his chosen, and that is supremely good.'

Charles H. Spurgeon[1]

---

1. C. H. Spurgeon, *Cheque Book of the Bank of Faith*, (Scotland: Christian Focus Publications, 1996), p. 149.

Mmm, Mmm Good!

One of my fondest boyhood memories comes from my mother's kitchen. My mom could cook. And she could bake. The woman was a Cajun Julia Child. One of her specialties was chocolate cake. I can see one now: three dinner-plate round, bronze colored layers, each about two inches tall, with mahogany brown icing, thick as paste, mortaring them and blanketing the whole; mother mixing the icing in a bowl then slathering it all over the cake with a wide white plastic knife; then handing me the bowl and a spoon to treat myself to the ribbon slivers of icing left on its sides and bottom. Like Campbell's soup, it was 'mmm, mmm good!'

The optimism about God that's faith is mmm, mmm good too. That's because when you're optimistic about Him He gives you pleasures you won't otherwise enjoy. It's these grace pleasures that make optimism about God so important. Here's the proposition: *When you're optimistic about God He'll do you great good.*

Jesus' dealings with the centurion we met earlier are like a bowl full of the icing of good things God will do for you when you're optimistic about Him. I give you five sweet slivers to help you 'taste and see that the Lord is good.'[2] Remember, as you lick the spoon, this is just the icing, not the cake. These are *examples* of the kind of good the Lord will do you when you are optimistic about Him. They in no way *exhaust* His generosity.

---

2. Psalm 34:8, 1 Peter 2:3.

I. One grace pleasure God will give you when you're optimistic about Him is *the good of helping you prevail over great problems.* Years ago when the going got tough for his Irish, Notre Dame Coach Frank Leahy wrote a one sentence motivational speech on the blackboard: 'When the going gets tough, the tough get going.' Here's the Christian version: 'God is at His best when life is at its worst.' Big problems are the Operating Room where the Great Physician displays His peerless surgical skills. You see this in the centurion's situation. His treasured servant is dying. But he prevails over this problem through optimism about Jesus. Eavesdrop on his self-talk: 'The Grim Reaper may have already written my servant's obituary and chiseled his name on a headstone but Jesus can erase both.' And Jesus greets his optimism with His prevailing help. Will He always remove your problems? No. But when you're optimistic about Him He will always give you what you need to handle any problem He doesn't remove. 'No temptation has overtaken you that is not common to man. God is faithful, and he will not let you be tempted beyond your ability but with the temptation he will also provide a way of escape, that you may be able to endure it.'[3] Read your Bible from cover to cover and you'll see the truth of this assurance. Again and again, when life is at its worst God is at His best for those who are optimistic about Him. When you're optimistic about God He will give you the good of helping you prevail over great problems.

---

3. 1 Corinthians 10:13.

II. A second good the Lord will do for you when you're optimistic about Him is the good of *answering big prayers*. If prayer is 'letting your requests be made known to God,'[4] then the centurion is praying. Get the message in this fact: *when you're optimistic about God you __will__ pray*. Say you love to fish. I invite you to fish with me in the Dead Sea. Will you? No. Why not? There's nothing to catch there. Change the venue. We go to a well-stocked pond where the fish are teenager hungry and always biting. You'll throw in your line won't you? Yes! Why? You fish where you know they're biting. And you'll throw your prayer line in when you're optimistic God's pond teems with answers. That's what makes the centurion cast in his lure. He's optimistic Jesus will help him. So he asks. Isn't this the way Jesus encourages you to pray? Doesn't He tell you, 'My Father's pond is stocked, His fish are always biting, throw in your line'? Isn't that what He means when He says, 'Ask and it shall be given'?[5] Optimism about God will make you pray.

The optimism that will make you pray will *make you pray big prayers*. Do you remember sitting on Santa's lap as a child? What did you ask for? Something big I bet. Why? Because you were optimistic Santa could deliver. This made you Santa-size your requests. You ought to be the same little child at the throne of grace. You ought to Father-size your askings. God wants you to ask for big things, the bigger the better. The centurion does! He doesn't fish for minnows; he fishes for marlin. He asks for the big thing of his servant's complete healing. And Jesus gives him what he asks. Again,

---

4. Philippians 4:6-7.

5. Matthew 7:7.

this doesn't mean God will always give you what you ask. What it means is there *are* great things available to you for the asking, far greater things than you imagine. Listen to your Father: 'Open your mouth wide and I will fill it.'[6] Listen to Paul: you pray to the One who 'is able to do far more abundantly than all that we ask or think.'[7] Listen to John Newton: 'Thou art coming to a King / Large petitions with thee bring / For his grace and power are such / None can ever ask too much.'[8] Bring large petitions to Him, Christian – the larger the better! When you do you will find the Lord giving you the good of answering your big prayers.

III. A third good God will give you when you're optimistic about Him is the good of *pleasing Him*. The movie *Hoosiers* is about the resurrection of a basketball coach's Lazarus career. Norman Dale is banned from college coaching for punching one of his players. After ten years in the Navy, a high school principal friend gives him the job of coaching the Hickory High School Huskers. The first person Dale meets at the school is English teacher, Myra Fleener. Dale later tells her he wanted to kiss her at that moment. The

---

6. Psalm 81:10. Commenting on this verse Calvin writes, 'He not only bids them open their mouth, but he magnifies the abundance of his grace still more highly, by intimating, that however enlarged our desires may be, there will be nothing wanting which is necessary to afford us full satisfaction. Whence it follows that the reason why God's blessings drop upon us in a sparing and slender manner is, because our mouth is too narrow ...' John Calvin, *Calvin's Commentary Volume 5*, (Grand Rapids, Michigan: Baker Book House, 1979 reprint), p. 320.

7. Ephesians 3:20.

8. John Newton, 'Come, My Soul, Thy Suit Prepare', stanza 2.

feeling wasn't mutual. By the movie's end this has changed. Dale is standing on the floor of the massive field house where the game was played, triumphantly hoisting the Indiana High School State Championship trophy. The crowd is thick as a New York subway car at rush hour. But Dale catches Myra's eye. She is beaming with love and pride. Her pleasure in Dale means more to him than the victory. I want Jesus to beam at me this way. I want Jesus to tell me, 'Charley, I'm pleased with you! Well done!' When I'm functioning sanely, I want this more than anything else.

How *do* I please Him? By being optimistic about Him. Don't you see this in the centurion? Jesus applauds his optimism.[9] It delights the Lord. Think of this. You may not be a Christian celebrity. *The New York Times* won't carry your obituary when you die. But if you live a life of optimism about God you'll please Him. In fact, every time you face any crisis, any struggle, any pain, any problem, any challenge with optimism about your Lord He beams with approval. There is nothing better than this. Nothing! I'd rather have Jesus' smile than Tiger Woods' Major Championships, Bill Gates' wealth, and Benedict Cumberbatch's good looks – combined! And I have His smile whenever I'm optimistic about Him, because this optimism is faith: and faith pleases Him![10] When you're optimistic about God He will do you the good of being pleased with you.

---

9. Matthew 8:10.
10. Hebrews 11:6.

IV. A fourth good the Lord will give you when you're optimistic about Him is the good of *allowing you to encourage others to be optimistic about Him*. The canons are roaring; the muskets are prodigally picking off men in greedy bunches. Fear is heavy as ammunition smoke. Rebel soldiers are panicking, their fight or flight systems flashing 'Flee!' But one man's system flashes 'Fight!' He refuses to take counsel of his fears. He holds his ground. General Bernard E. Bee spots him and rallies his men with words that leave this courageous officer with the nickname he still bears, like initials in a driveway long after the carver is gone. 'Look, men, there is Jackson standing like a stone wall.'[11] The sight of Thomas J. Jackson's gallantry releases in Bee's men the adrenalin of courage. They turn; they fight; they win. This is the power of example. It's stronger than a nuclear bomb, more contagious than the flu. That's one reason this centurion's story is in the Bible.[12] The Holy Spirit tells you about him to infect you with the happy virus of optimism. His story does that doesn't it? Don't you find it half-time pep talk rousing? Doesn't his example, and Jesus' response, encourage you to be optimistic about your Savior? The wonder of wonders is, when you're optimistic about God others will hoist their kites in your wind. You'll be their Stonewall Jackson. And that's good. It's a good the Lord will gladly do you when you are optimistic about Him.

---

11. Steve Wilkins, *All Things for Good*, (Nashville, Tennessee: Cumberland House Publishing, 2004), p. 89.

12. Romans 15:4.

V. A fifth good the Lord will do you when you are optimistic about Him is the supreme good of *allowing you to honor Him*. I frequently counsel people. They enter my office with shoulders drooping like tree limbs blanketed by heavy snow. They open closets full of skeletons and tell me things that defeat them, shame them, and strangle their souls. Before they begin, I say, 'I want to tell you something before you tell me anything. I want to tell you, "Thank you".' I typically get a 'What's wrong with this guy?' look. Then I explain. 'Thank you for trusting me enough to tell me your truth. Your trust honors me.' I mean that. When someone trusts me enough to ask for my help that person is saying, 'Charley, I see you as someone with integrity, compassion, and wisdom.' And that honors me.

The centurion demonstrates that when you're optimistic about Jesus you honor Him as a counselee does his counselor. This man's optimism about Jesus is 'a thousand tongues' singing 'our great Redeemer's praise.' It confesses that Jesus is so good and so great that nothing is too hard for Him. This exalts our Lord.

You want to honor Jesus don't you? You know that whatever you do is to be done for His glory.[13] Here's the main way you can do that. No – that's not a misprint, not an exaggeration. Being optimistic about the Lord isn't just *a* way of honoring Him.[14] It's *the* way. Ultimately, all other

---

13. 1 Corinthians 10:31.

14. For example, *patience* in trial honors the Lord. But what is patience except endurance born of optimism that the Lord is in control and is working for your good? *Praise* honors God. What fuels praise? The optimism that calls on God for help, experiences His help, and returns to worship and thank Him for his kindness. *Faith* honors God. And what is faith? It's optimism about God. Optimism about God is the root of every God honoring thought, word, and deed.

ways of glorifying Him are rays from this sun. Isn't this breathtaking? The simple childlike faith that's optimism about God allows you, a frail creature of dust and feeble as frail, to honor Him. Truly, His thoughts are not our thoughts, and His ways are not our ways. You see that in this fact that when you're optimistic about Him, He does you the supreme good of allowing you to honor Him.

Christian, here are five examples of the pleasures God will give you when you are optimistic about Him. Sweet as these grapes from the grace vine are, there are plenty more waiting to be plucked with the hand of optimism. Doesn't this encourage you to begin living by the Grace Paradigm?

Doesn't the good God will do you if you live by the Grace Paradigm make you want to shift to it? Make that shift now, Christian. Make it and you'll begin tasting God's Grace Pleasures.

They're Mmm, Mmm Good!

Paradigm Shift II

6

A Grace Primer
Nine Reasons Grace Gives You To Be Optimistic About God

'No need in Christendom is more urgent than the need for a renewed awareness of what the grace of God really is. Christians long to see reformation and renewal in the churches; today as yesterday, it is only from a rediscovery of grace that these blessings will flow.'[1]

J. I. Packer

Primer: 'A book that covers the basic elements of a subject.'[2]

---

1. J. I. Packer, *God's Words*, (Downers Grove, Illinois: InterVarsity Press, 1981), p. 96.

2. http://www.the free dictionary.com/primer

Son, Don't You Know the Meaning of Grace?

If you had been there when it happened, you would have reacted the way we did. Startled. Stunned. Scared. *There* was the sanctuary of Westminster Presbyterian Church, Jackson, Mississippi. *It* was what my alma mater called 'sermon criticism.' This was a euphemism for the emotional waterboarding of preaching a sermon to your classmates and professors then enduring a critique by several of the faculty.

A classmate preached. A professor was critiquing. Even in those days when self-esteem wasn't esteemed, the prof's first words struck like a heart attack. 'Son, don't you know the meaning of grace?'

Now, we didn't know much. We sure didn't know as much as we thought we knew. But we knew enough to know that question was a warden's steps echoing down the corridor, coming to fetch our friend for a date with a firing squad. He got no last meal. No final smoke. No blindfold. Just a bullet between his eyes.

Forget that sermon doctor's less than appealing bedside manner. Focus on his question. It highlights an important point about grace and optimism. Grace gives you reason to be optimistic about God every day, all day long. But there's an 'if' string attached. The *if* of understanding. *You must understand grace to be optimistic about God every day, all day long.*

You can profit from many things without understanding them. You can ingest two Advil and enjoy their pain-evicting benefits without grasping their chemical makeup. Your doctor can replenish your fluids with a drip when you're dehydrated. It'll do its job even though you can't pronounce its contents. You can drive your car without a mechanic's engine expertise. But grace isn't like that. The grace perspective of optimism only survives and thrives in the habitat of understanding. You must understand grace if you're going to live with the optimism about God He wants you to have.

I. Too many Christians understand grace as *nothing more than forgiveness*. Forgiveness is glorious. It's foundational. But it's only one masterpiece hanging next to many others in the grace gallery. You betray a serious misunderstanding of grace if you don't see that. And many don't see it. I know I didn't for a long time.

Imagine someone visiting a famous art gallery exhibiting the world's 100 greatest paintings. On one wall are Rembrandt's 'Mona Lisa', Leonardo's 'The Last Supper', and Michelangelo's 'Universal Judgment'. Another wall houses Dali's 'Persistence of Memory' and Van Gogh's 'Starry Night'. On and on it goes as everywhere this patron turns an artistic burning bush beckons. But he doesn't turn. He sits and stares at only one of the paintings as if there were only one wall and only one painting. And the patron does this again and again, day after day.

I was that patron. I visited the grace gallery and sat before its forgiveness masterpiece as if it were the only painting hanging. I knew I was forgiven—'justified' to use the theological word. And that exhausted my grasp of grace. Because of my limited understanding, grace didn't amaze me. It didn't inspire me. It didn't make me optimistic about God in my everyday living.

Maybe you see yourself in my mirror. Maybe your understanding of grace is as narrow as mine was. If it is, I gladly share with you what I've found. I've found that grace is far more than forgiveness. And I've found something grander: *everything grace is gives you reason to be optimistic about God.* So, the more you understand grace, the more reasons you'll have to be a Grace-Focused Optimist.

II. One way to understand something is through a *primer.* A primer gives you a subject's primary ideas.[3] Section II is a *Grace Primer.* It gives you in compact, portable form the Bible's primary grace teachings. Understanding grace through the Grace Primer is the second Paradigm shift you must go through if you're going to live the way God wants you to as a Grace-Focused Optimist.

The core of God's grace message is found in nine truths. Each of these gives you reason to be optimistic about God.

1. *God's Grace Policy:* Grace gives you reason to be optimistic about God because His policy is to be gracious with you all the time.

2. *God's Grace Plan:* Grace gives you reason to be optimistic about God because His plan is to exalt Himself by humbling Himself to exalt you.

3. The *Grace Position:* Grace gives you reason to be optimistic about God because, through Jesus' righteousness, He accepts you even though you do unacceptable things.

---

3. Linguists say that primer comes from the Latin word meaning 'primary.' www.miriam-webster./com/primer

4. The *Grace Privilege*: Grace gives you reason to be optimistic about God because He makes much of being your Father and wants you to make much of being His child.

5. *Grace Providence*: Grace gives you reason to be optimistic about God because His providence assures you that everything that happens to you is from Him and for your good.

6. *Grace Promises*: Grace gives you reason to be optimistic about God because His promises arm you to live for Him, especially when you find it hard to do so.

7. *Grace Provision*: Grace gives you reason to be optimistic about God because He will provide all your needs.

8. *Grace Power*: Grace gives you reason to be optimistic about God because He will empower you to live for Him by love.

9. *Grace Perfection*: Grace gives you reason to be optimistic about God because your ultimate perfection is assured by His tying His reputation to perfecting you.

III. There's a caveat. You can know grace well enough to discuss it with John Calvin, yet not live with optimism about God. That's because living optimistically because of grace is like writing a book. It takes more than knowing the meaning of words to write. Many people are walking thesauruses. They know words from their cognate families to their distant synonym cousins. They can finish the *New York Times* crossword puzzle quickly. But they can't put these words together in syntactic beauty. They can't write. It's the same with the grace manuscript of optimism. Having a Noah Webster grasp of the meaning of the nine grace truths won't make you an Ernest Hemingway. More is needed.

The more needed is *personal*. You need the Holy Spirit's help. Like a skillful editor, He can help you turn grace words into the grace prose of optimistic living. Thankfully, securing the Spirit's help isn't hard. His expertise is yours for the asking. Jesus assures you, 'If you then, who are evil, know how to give good gifts to your children, how much more will the heavenly Father give the Holy Spirit to those who ask him.'[4]

So, *ask*. Ask your way through each of the following chapters. Ask for an Emmaus Road heart. Ask the Spirit to open the Scriptures to you and you to the Scriptures. Ask for a heart burning with optimism as the Spirit talks to you about the fullness of grace that's yours in Jesus.[5] Ask! Ask! Ask!

Then, *expect*. Be the way you are when you order a book from Amazon. You expect the book to come in the mail. So expect the Spirit to use His Word's grace teaching to make you the optimist God wants you to be.

If you ask and expect, *you can be optimistic that God by grace will make you optimistic about Him*. And you'll be able

---

4. Luke 11:13.

5. Luke 24:13-35.

to answer the question, 'Don't you know the meaning of grace?' with 'Yes, by God's grace I do!'

7

God's Grace Policy
The *First* Reason Grace Gives You to Be Optimistic About God

'Finally, the Christian under grace is free from bondage to fear (Rom. 8:15ff.; cf. 1 John. 4:17 ff.) – fear, that is, of the unknown future, or of meeting God (as one day we must all do), or of being destroyed by hostile forces or horrific experiences of one sort or another. He knows himself to be God's child, adopted, beloved, secure, with his inheritance awaiting him and eternal joy guaranteed. He knows that nothing can separate him from the love of God in Christ, nor dash him from his Saviour's hand, and *that nothing can happen to him which is not for his long-term good, making him more like Jesus and bringing him ultimately closer to God.* So when fears flood his soul, as they do the soul of every normal person from time to time, he drives them back by reminding himself of these things ... .'[1]

J. I. Packer

'Dejection in the godly arises from a double spring; either because their inward comforts are darkened, or their outward comforts are disturbed. To cure both these troubles, ... would prescribe them to take, now and then, a little of this Cordial: ALL THINGS WORK TOGETHER FOR GOOD TO THEM THAT LOVE GOD. To know that nothing hurts the godly, is a matter of comfort; but to be assured that all things which fall out shall co-operate for their good, that their crosses shall be turned into blessings, that showers of affliction water the withering root of their grace and make it flourish more; this may fill their hearts with joy till they run over.'[2]

Thomas Watson

Tout Est Grace!

The school I serve has a handbook. It's a policy manual. It tells faculty, students, and parents the school's policy – its way of handling things – on everything from honor code violations to dress requirements. The Bible tells you God has a policy manual He follows in all His dealings with you. It's called grace. God's Grace Policy with you gives you the first reason you should be optimistic about Him. The proposition is, *God's Grace Policy is His choice to be good to you in all His dealings with you.*

---

1. J. I. Packer, *God's Words* (Downers Grove, Illinois: InterVarsity Press, 1981), p. 107. Emphasis added.

2. Thomas Watson, *All Things For Good* (Edinburgh: The Banner of Truth Trust, 1986 reprint), p. 8.

I. God has *chosen* you. You are one of 'God's elect.'[3] God chose you in Christ 'before the foundation of the world.'[4] He didn't choose you because you were a first round draft choice, among the best and the brightest, a person of beauty or brilliance. Like me, you had no form or comeliness distinguishing you from those not chosen. None of the chosen are choice.[5] You were no different than those God leaves in their sin. He could have left you, too, without wronging you. Neither did God choose you because in the crystal ball of His perfect knowledge He saw that you'd believe the Gospel. In fact, if God had not chosen you, you would never have chosen Him. Your faith in Jesus is the child, not the parent, of His choice.[6] God chose you for one reason and only one reason. God chose you because He chose to choose you. The reason He chose to choose you is found in Him not in you. To be sure, many denounce this truth as unfair, even monstrous. Others ignore it as if it's irrelevant to godly living. The Apostle Paul is not one of these. He praises God for choosing him.[7] He does that because he knows if God hadn't chosen him he would never have chosen Christ. And he knows that election is the mouth of the

3. 1 Peter 1:1. Wayne Grudem defines election as 'an act of God before creation in which he chooses some people to be saved, not on account of any foreseen merit in them, but only because of his sovereign good pleasure.' Wayne Grudem, *Systematic Theology: An Introduction to Biblical Doctrine* (Grand Rapids, Michigan: Zondervan, 1994), p. 670.

4. Ephesians 1:4; Acts 13:48; Romans 8:28-30; Romans 9:11-13; 1 Thessalonians 1:4-5.

5. Romans 9:11-18.

6. Acts 13:48.

7. Ephesians 1:3-4.

river of grace. Join Paul. Praise God for 'the glory of his grace'[8] to you in choosing you.

II. God has chosen you *as someone to whom He will be good*. The New Testament's one sentence biography of Jesus is 'He went around doing good.'[9] That same sentence sums up God's grace policy with you. He says to you what He said to Abraham: 'I will bless you.'[10] He makes the same promise to you that He made to Jacob: 'I will do you good.'[11] The good He has done, is doing, and will continue doing you is His *best* good. It's the good of blessing you with every spiritual blessing.[12] It's the good of making you His heir.[13] It's the good of being your Father and He is the best of fathers.[14] It's the good of being your Shepherd and He is the best of shepherds.[15] It's the good of being your Friend and He is the best of friends.[16] It's the good of being your Helper and He is the best of helpers.[17] It's the good of being your 'shield and your very great reward' and He is the best of shields and the greatest of rewards.[18] In sum, God will do you the good of making you perfectly

---

8. Ephesians 1:6, 12, 14.

9. Acts 10:38.

10. Genesis 12:2.

11. Genesis 32:9.

12. Ephesians 1:3-14.

13. Galatians 4:7.

14. Galatians 4:6; Matthew 7:7-11; Luke 11:13.

15. Psalm 23.

16. John 15:15.

17. Hebrews 13:5-6.

18. Genesis 15:1.

and permanently like Jesus.[19] By doing that He'll make you perfectly and permanently happy. And that's the best good He can do you!

III. God has chosen you as someone to whom He will be good *all the time*. J. R. R. Tolkien coined the word 'eucatastrophe' by adding the prefix *eu* to the word catastrophe. 'Eu' means 'good.' A eucatastrophe is something very bad turning out very good.[20] God's choice of you assures you that even your catastrophes are eucatastrophes. Even in them He is up to your good.[21] Even the worst things that happen to you will 'advance the gospel' in your life in the sense of making you more like your Savior.[22] Like Joseph you will be able to name even your worst experiences 'Ephraim' as you say 'God has made me fruitful in the land of my affliction.'[23] Your testimony at the end will be 'Surely goodness and mercy have followed *me* all the days of my life and *I* shall dwell in the house of the Lord forever.'[24]

IV. God's choice to be good to you all the time is *the reason He brought you into existence*. You aren't a bottle washed ashore the beach of existence by the high tide of chance. Evolution didn't shape you from the dust of

---

19. Romans 8:29; 1 John 3:2.

20. Brad Brewer, *Mentored by the King* (Grand Rapids, Michigan: Zondervan, 2010), p. 138.

21. Romans 8:28; Hebrews 12:5-13.

22. Philippians 1:12.

23. Genesis 41:52.

24. Psalm 23:6. Emphasis added.

the ground and breathe into your nostrils the breath of life. You exist because the God who 'gives to all mankind life and breath and everything' created you.[25] And He created you for the sole purpose of being good to you. Paul is speaking of you when he talks about men and women 'called according to God's purpose.'[26] He leaves you in no doubt what God's purpose is: 'For those whom he foreknew he also predestined to be conformed to the image of his Son, in order that he might be the firstborn among many brothers. And those whom he predestined he also called, and those whom he called he also justified, and those whom he justified he also glorified.'[27] What does this mean? It means nothing less than the mind-blowing, heart-exhilarating, praise-producing fact that you exist solely, wholly, and only because God is determined to be good to you.

V. God's choice to be good to you all the time *is strikingly displayed in being good to you in the time between your birth and new birth.* You deprive God of deserved praise if you overlook the good He did you in your unsaved condition. Then He did you the good of *not allowing you to die a Christless death.* In the stark words of Jesus many 'die in their sins.'[28] Like the Egyptians without blood on their doorposts, the avenging angel strikes them in their unforgiven state. The split second they die they step into eternal misery. But that didn't

---

25. Acts 17:25.

26. Romans 8:28.

27. Romans 8:29-30.

28. John 8:24.

happen to you. Why not? Because God was following a grace policy with you even then. Again, God did you the good of *not allowing your heart to become hardened in your resistance to Him* during this time. Your unbelieving days may have been days of walking in the counsel of the ungodly, standing in the way of sinners, and sitting in the seat of scoffers.[29] But you never became Pharaoh-hard.[30] Why not? Or maybe you had parents as godly as Timothy's grandmother and mother, Lois and Eunice.[31] They modeled and messaged faith in Jesus to you, trained you in the way you should go, brought you to a church where Christ crucified was preached with passion and power. In spite of these privileges, you refused to believe. Yet you never became wayside soil impervious.[32] Why not? The only thing that kept you from being permanently hardened in your rejection of Jesus was the fact that God was following a grace policy with you even then. God did you one other good at that time: *He didn't allow you to commit the unforgiveable sin.* There is one. Jesus calls it "blasphemy against the Spirit."[33] Some have committed spiritual suicide by sinning this way. But you didn't. Why not? For one reason and one only: God was following a grace policy with you even in your unsaved days.

I confess that I find it hard to write another sentence. Not because of writer's block. Because of worship block. The sole reason God created me was to be good to me.

29. Psalm 1:1.

30. Exodus 8:32.

31. 2 Timothy 1:5; Proverbs 22:6.

32. Matthew 13:4.

33. Matthew 12:31.

And He was good to me even before I became a Christian. In John Newton's words: 'Determined to save, he watched o'er my path, while Satan's blind slave, I sported with death.'[34] These thoughts make me sing with Moses, dance with Miriam, express gratitude with the returning leper, and magnify the Lord with Mary.[35] Don't they tune your heart to sing His grace with songs of loudest praise too?

VI. God's choice to be good to you all the time *brought the gospel to you*. A pagan general named Naaman gets leprosy. One of his domestic servants – a young girl – tells him about the prophet Elisha. God uses Elisha to bring Naaman to true religion. A fascinating story. But it's not primarily about Namaan or the servant girl or Elisha. It's about God. About how He brings the gospel to people. Look again at this girl. How was she brought to Naaman? She was a military spoil of his conquest of Israel. Listen to the report of Naaman's victory: 'Naaman, commander of the army of the king of Syria, was a great man with his master and in high favor, because by him *the Lord had given victory to Syria.*'[36] You see, *God* brought to Naaman the girl who brought the gospel to him. He's done something similar with you. Some servant girl – a Christian parent, a sermon, a tract, a friend's testimony – told you about Jesus. Let this be a speed bump slowing you down. You heard about Jesus. Millions never have; millions never will. But you have. Why? God's grace!

---

34. John Newton, 'Begone Unbelief', stanza 4.

35. Exodus 15; Luke 17:16; Luke 1:46-55.

36. Naaman's story is told in 2 Kings 5:1-19.

Listen to Paul: 'How then will they call on him whom they have not believed? And how are they to believe in him of whom they have never heard? And how are they to hear without someone preaching? And how are they to preach unless they are sent? As it is written, 'How beautiful are the feet of those who preach the good news.'[37] Beautiful feet walked into your life because God sent them. You heard the gospel because God brought it to you. And God brought it to you because of His grace policy toward you.

VII. God's grace policy with you *brought you to the gospel*. A cowboy hears a motivational speaker say, 'You can lead a horse to water but you can't make him drink.' The talk over, the cowboy tells him, 'I enjoyed what you said but you're wrong about being unable to make a horse drink. Just put salt in his oats – that'll make him drink!' God in grace didn't just bring you to the living water; He put salt in your oats. He made you drink. God's salt is a compound made up of regeneration and conversion. He *gave you spiritual life*. You were born a spiritual corpse in Adam's cemetery.[38] Left to yourself you'd still be in your tomb. You'd still be without hope and without God in the world.[39] You'd still be on the broad path leading to destruction.[40] Left to yourself you could no more give yourself spiritual life than a physically dead person can give himself physical life. Left to yourself you could not see the kingdom or enter it.[41] Left to yourself you saw no

---

37. Romans 10:14-16.
38. Romans 5:12. Psalms 51:5.
39. Ephesians 2:12.
40. Matthew 6:13.
41. John 3:3, 5.

need of Jesus, had no desire for Jesus, couldn't and wouldn't take one step toward Jesus. But God didn't leave you to yourself. God made you another Lazarus. God brought you from your spiritual grave. God gave you life. God made you alive to the significance of Jesus. God 'who said, "Let light shine out of darkness," has shone in our hearts to give the light of the knowledge of the glory of God in the face of Jesus Christ.'[42] You've been born again.[43]

Maybe this happened for you with sunrise quietness. From childhood you've had the blessing of being acquainted with the sacred writings which are able to make you wise for salvation through faith in Jesus Christ.[44] Your first lullaby was 'Jesus loves me this I know, for the Bible tells me so.' You can't remember a time when you weren't trusting Jesus. Still, at some point, even though you can't cite a time on the clock or a date on the calendar, God made you alive in Jesus. Or maybe God made you alive to the significance of Jesus with Damascus Road vividness. Your testimony's the line in the hymn, 'Years I spent in vanity and pride / caring not my Lord was crucified.'[45] Maybe you neglected Him completely. Maybe you thought you knew Him but didn't. Then, as suddenly as a blink, you saw Jesus as He really is, the Son of God and Savior of the world, full of grace and truth, the one thing worth everything, your Lord and your God. And you wanted Him more than anything. What happened? Regeneration. New birth.

42. 2 Corinthians 4:6.

43. John 3:7.

44. 2 Timothy 3:15.

45. William R. Newell, 'At Calvary', stanza 1.

God gave you life![46] And He gave you life because His policy toward you is grace.

The Lord then enabled you to rest entirely on Jesus for your acceptance by God. All your soul's investments are in Jesus' stock. You have no righteousness but His righteousness. You have no plea but His blood. If he turns out a Bear Market you'll be eternally bankrupt. He won't. He is the Bull Market that'll never crash. You are safe in Him. And this disposition of rest on Jesus is faith. At its core, this faith is optimism about God, confidence that He'll keep His great gospel promise, 'Believe in the Lord Jesus and you will be saved.'[47] Your faith is *yours*. It's as personal as your DNA. It's your act. It's your choice. But your act is *God's* gift.[48] Your faith is 'the faith of God's elect.'[49] And He gave you faith because His policy toward you is grace.

VIII. This fact that you are a Christian is *God's assurance to you that He is following a grace policy in all His dealings with you.* Since you wouldn't have become a Christian without God bringing the gospel to you and you to the gospel; and since the *only* people God does this with are those He includes in His grace policy; then,

---

46. John 3:3,5; Ephesians 2:1-10. There are variations between the poles of not knowing the time of regeneration and the 'I can remember it as though it happened yesterday' experience of regeneration. The issue isn't 'Does my experience fit one or the other?' The issue is, 'Am I alive?' And the answer to that is 'Do I trust Jesus alone for my rightness with God?' Faith isn't the *cause* of regeneration; it's the *effect* and, consequently, the *evidence* that new birth has occurred.

47. Acts 16:31.

48. Ephesians 2:8-10; Philippians 1:29; Acts 13:48.

49. Titus 1:1.

your becoming a Christian is both the *effect* and *evidence* that God has chosen to include you in His grace policy. Your conversion is the equivalent of God opening His grace book, that 'family Bible' of the redeemed, the 'book of life,' the massive volume filled with the names of 'a great multitude that no man can number';[50] running His finger down a column until He stops at a name and taps it several times while saying to you, 'Child, look at this'; and you look and, O praise His Name!, you see *your* name written in His perfect script with the indelible ink of His choice.[51] You see this link between God's grace policy and becoming a Christian everywhere in the New Testament. You can think about it like this: *conversion (being a Christian) evidences inclusion (in God's grace policy)*. Take two for instances.

Paul tells the 'Thessalonians' he is sure God's policy toward them is grace: 'For we know, brothers loved by God, that he has chosen you.' What makes him sure is they're Christians: '… because our gospel came to you not only in word, but also in power and in the Holy Spirit and with full conviction … and you turned to God from idols to serve the living and true God, and to wait for his Son from heaven, whom he raised from the dead, Jesus who delivers us from the wrath to come.'[52] You see, conversion (being a Christian) evidences inclusion (in God's grace policy).

---

50. Revelation 7:9.

51. Revelation 20:12.

52. 1 Thessalonians 1:4-5; 9-10.

Paul makes the same point to the 'Ephesians'. He is sure God's policy toward them is grace. 'Blessed be the God and Father of our Lord Jesus Christ, who has blessed us in Christ with every spiritual blessing in the heavenly places, even as he chose us in him before the foundation of the world.' What makes him sure is they're Christians: 'In him you also, when you heard the word of truth, the gospel of your salvation, and believed in him, were sealed with the promised Holy Spirit, who is the guarantee of our inheritance until we acquire possession of it, to the praise of his glory.'[53] You see, conversion (being a Christian) evidences inclusion (in God's grace policy).[54]

God's linking of conversion (being a Christian) with inclusion (being in His grace policy) underlines the wonder of being a Christian. It's why being a Christian ought to amaze, thrill, inspire, encourage, comfort, excite, satisfy, and empower you. Being a Christian means God has included you in His grace policy. It means you are a Grace Person!

As you will see in the remainder of *the Grace Primer* section, as someone included in God's grace policy, *all that happens to you is grace.* I love the way Georges Bernanos puts this in *The Diary of a Country Priest.* It's the story of a young French priest serving a rural parish. We aren't told his name. We're simply allowed to look over his shoulder and read his diary. It's not an easy read, especially if you're a pastor. The poor *padre* is a mess. Spiritually, he struggles with whether he should be a priest. Socially, he

---

53. Ephesians 1:3-4, 13-14.

54. Other examples are: John 17:2; 1 Corinthians 1:26-30; Acts 13:46.

is a walking *faux pas*. Relationally, his interaction with his parishioners evokes their disdain. Yet he faithfully shepherds them. All the while (unknown to him and them), he's suffering from stomach cancer. At the end of the book he lies dying on a friend's bed. The friend sends for the local priest. He isn't going to arrive in time. I'll allow the friend to tell you the rest: 'The priest was still on his way, and finally I was bound to voice my deep regret that such delay threatened to deprive my comrade of the final consolations of our Church. He did not seem to hear me. But a few moments later he put his hand over mine, and his eyes entreated me to draw closer to him. He then uttered these words almost in my ear. And I am quite sure that I have recorded them accurately, for his voice, though halting, was strangely distinct. "Does it matter? All is grace. ..." I think he died just then.'[55]

Tout est grâce: all is grace! John Calvin couldn't say it better. *Tout est grâce*, Christian. Your delights are grace, your disappointments are grace; your pleasures are grace, your pains are grace; your triumphs are grace, your tragedies are grace. You can bookend whatever happens to you with Joseph's 'God meant it for good'[56]

---

55. Georges Bernanos, *The Diary of a Country Priest* (Cambridge, MA: Da Capo Press, 1937), p. 298. I thank my sister in Christ, Irene Marxsen, French teacher at FPD, for translating the final paragraph of Bernanos' book for me.

56. Genesis 50:20. Calvin comments on this verse, 'Let the impious busy themselves as they please, let them rage, let them mingle heaven and earth; yet they shall gain nothing by their ardor; and not only shall their impetuosity prove ineffectual, but shall be turned to an issue the reverse of that which they intended, so that they shall promote our salvation, though they do it reluctantly. So that whatever poison Satan produces, God turns it into medicine for his elect.' www.studylight.org/commentary/genesis/50-20.html

and Paul's 'all things work together for good to them that love God, to them that are the called according to his purpose.'[57] This is the message of grace. Grace is God's policy with you. God's Grace Policy with you assures you He has chosen to be good to you in all His dealings with you.

Doesn't this give you reason to be optimistic about God?

---

57. Romans 8:28.

8

God's Grace Plan
The *Second* Reason Grace Gives You To Be Optimistic About God

'Our greatest hindrance in living the Christian life is not our lack of effort but our lack of acquaintance with our privileges.'

John Owen[1]

'It should cause us great joy to know that it is the purpose of God the Father, Son, and Holy Spirit to give of themselves to us to bring us true joy and happiness. It is God's nature to act that way toward those upon whom he has set his love, and he will continue to act that way toward us for all eternity.'

Wayne Grudem[2]

---

1. Ian Hamilton, *The Cross of Christ*, a lecture given at the Inverness Branch of the Scottish Reformation Society, Monday, 14 November, 2005.

2. Wayne Grudem, *Systematic Theology: An Introduction to Biblical Doctrine*, (Grand Rapids, Michigan: Zondervan, 1994), p. 199.

The Fairy Tale Ending That's Not a Fairy Tale

That's NOT what it is. I know it's the accepted definition. The party line. But the first thing to know about grace is that it's *not* 'God giving you the opposite of what you deserve.' This definition whittles God's California Redwood forest down to a box of toothpicks. And it's about as thrilling as finding a penny on the sidewalk. That understanding of grace isn't amazing.

What makes grace amazing is what grace IS. It's God's Plan. His Grace Plan gives you the second reason you should be optimistic about God. We can put this truth like this: God's grace plan gives you reason to be optimistic about Him because *Grace is God exalting Himself by humbling Himself to exalt you.*

I. Grace is God's plan to *exalt* you.[3] John tells you your future: 'He shall wipe away every tear from their eyes, and death shall be no more, neither shall there be mourning, nor crying, nor pain anymore, for the former things have passed away.'[4] One word accurately describes being in a place where death is dead and tears, mourning, crying, and pain are *persona non grata*: happiness.[5]

---

3. I use 'exalt' to sum up the message of verses telling us what God has in mind for believers. See, for example, Acts 3:21; Romans 8:18-24; 1 Corinthians 15:35-57; 2 Corinthians 5:1-5; Ephesians 1:9-12; Philippians 3:20-21.

4. Revelation 21:4.

5. We are leery of talking about happiness. We have been told, 'God isn't interested in your happiness. He is interested in your holiness.' But this is to put asunder what God joins together. God's interest in our holiness is by definition His interest in our happiness. Holiness is happiness! The holier I am the happier I'll be. For God to make me holy, then, is for God to make

God is going to make you *happy*. You're going to live with Jesus on the new earth.[6] You will enjoy unadulterated, uninhibited, unfettered, unbounded, unlimited, unbridled ecstasy. Your top ten earthly experiences of peak pleasure and 'I hope this moment never ends' delight will seem like a root canal without Novocain compared to the happiness God has in store for you.

God is going to make you *perfectly* happy. He is going to wipe away 'all' tears. I'm sure your cheeks are no strangers to tears. Health tears. Business tears. Family tears. But you're headed to tearlessness. There's no Kleenex where you're going. No hospitals or cemeteries. No police cars, fire stations, jails, or armies either. There'll be no need for them. Sorrow, sickness, sadness, surgery, and suffering will be replaced by happiness. You'll be *spiritually* happy. You'll be *emotionally* happy. You'll be *physically* happy. You'll be *socially* happy. You'll be *environmentally* happy. You're going to be perfectly happy.

God is going to make you *permanently* happy. Yours won't be school holiday happiness. As a teacher I look

---

me happy. J. I. Packer highlights the point: 'Happiness ... will be enjoyed in heaven.' Revelation 7:16-17 shows that. When glorified with Christ our condition will be one of conscious joy and whole-hearted delight in everything around (happiness at its highest), not simply of quiet contentment with the way things are (happiness at its lowest). But there is a catch. Heaven is a state of holiness, which only persons with holy tastes will appreciate, and into which only persons of holy character can enter (Rev. 21:27; 22:14). Accordingly, God's present purpose is to work holiness—which means Christlikeness—into us to fit us for heaven. *It is precisely God's concern for our future happiness that leads him to concentrate here and now on making us holy, for 'without holiness no one will see the Lord.'* J. I. Packer, *Hot Tub Religion*, (Wheaton, Illinois: Tyndale House Publishers, Inc., 1998), pp. 79-80. Emphasis added.

6. 2 Peter 3:13; Matthew 5:5; Revelation 21:1-4.

forward to them. Thanksgiving ... the season to be jolly ... Spring Break. Each passes quicker than a blink. I say to my wife, 'This week sure went by fast.' You won't say that about your coming happiness. John Newton nailed it: 'When you've been there ten thousand years, bright shining as the sun, you've no less days to sing God's praise, then when you first began.' You're going to be permanently happy.

God is out to exalt you.

THIS IS GRACE!

II. Grace is God exalting you by *humbling Himself.* A Mississippi lawyer once gently admonished me to lower my pulpit volume with these wise words: 'Charley, you can shout without ever raising your voice. Just choose the right word.'

Paul shouts about grace with the choice of right words. He roars in 2 Corinthians 8:9: 'For you know the *grace* of our Lord Jesus Christ, *that though he was rich, yet for our sake he became poor,* so that we by his poverty might become rich.' He raises the decibel level to rock concert height in Philippians 2:5-11 by telling us that though Jesus 'was in the form of God he did not count equality with God a thing to be grasped, *but made himself nothing, taking the form of a servant, being born in the likeness of men.* And being found in human form, *he humbled himself by becoming obedient to the point of death, even death on a cross.'*

These words emphasize *Jesus' dignity.* He was 'rich,' sharing 'equality with God.' God's glory, greatness, and gladness were His. When you look at Jesus you look at

God. When you look at Jesus you look at God acting in *grace*, personally and directly.[7]

At the heart of God's grace is God's *humbling himself.* Grace is God in the Person of His Son moving from conception to infancy to adolescence to adulthood with all their East of Eden serpent-in-every-garden challenges. Grace is the One who needs nothing, the source and sustainer of everything, becoming a helpless babe needing constant care. Grace is the Keeper of Israel, who neither slumbers nor sleeps, being kept as He slumbers and sleeps. Grace is the One who holds the seas in his hand being rocked in the arms of His mother and experiencing the infant realities of Gerbers and Pampers, cutting teeth and drooling, runny noses and earaches. Grace is the One before whom Seraphim cover their faces having no form or majesty that we should look at Him, and no beauty that we should desire Him. Grace is wisdom incarnate with relatives wishing to institutionalize Him in a psychiatric hospital. Grace is the One greater than the strong man binding Him and spoiling His goods only to have the religious authorities spin it as an inside job. Grace is God reviled as an imposter; excoriated as a blasphemer; betrayed by a disciple; abandoned by His friends; then crucified as though He were the worst man who ever lived. Grace is God hanging naked on a cross between two thieves before reaching the nadir of humiliation in the darkness of God's unmitigated judgment. Grace is the One who knew nothing but His Father's smile buried alive

---

7. John 14:9: 'Whoever has seen me has seen the Father.' Colossians 1:15: 'He is the image of the invisible God.' Hebrews 1:3: 'He is the radiance of the glory of God and the exact imprint of his nature.'

in the claustrophobic horror of God's curse against sin. Grace is God the Son crying to God the Father, 'My God, my God, why have you forsaken me?' And, my brother in Christ, my believing sister – grace is the answer to Jesus' question: because *you* are the answer. And, thank God, so am *I*. 'For our sake he made him to be sin who knew no sin, so that in him we might become the righteousness of God.'[8] Which, being interpreted, means Jesus is God humbling Himself to exalt us.

THIS IS GRACE!

III. Grace is God *exalting Himself* by humbling Himself to exalt you. Paul says Jesus' humbling of Himself to exalt you springs from and leads to 'the glory of God the Father.'[9]

Imagine a broken Stradivarius in the hands of Itzhak Perlman, the violinist. Imagine Itzhak has arthritic fingers. Imagine his stiff fingers coaxing beautiful music from his wounded instrument. That's life in this fallen world. It's a broken instrument. You have sin-stiffened fingers. Yet you have ample opportunities to play sweet music. Everywhere you turn – science, literature, music, sports, relationships and a thousand other places – you find opportunities to use your intellect, imagination, abilities, and powers. Surely this is a microcosm of life in the perfect world. Surely the new earth will be a place where healthy fingers play perfect instruments. Surely the new earth will be a place where everything you're capable

8. 2 Corinthians 5:21.

9. Philippians 2:11.

of doing and enjoying will be given infinite opportunity for free and full exercise. All without fatigue, jading, boredom, or discontent. Only day after day after day of discovery and delight, pleasure and profit, friendship and fellowship. Narnia under the White Witch's reign was 'always winter but never Christmas.' The new earth will be always summer *and* always Christmas. Your gracious God will give you grace present after grace present. Best of all, He will inundate you with the wonder of what He is.[10]

When this time comes *God will be exalted*. This is His *goal* in everything He will have done from creation to consummation. From start to finish He has been determined to 'make known the riches of his glory.'[11] His saving actions through Jesus aimed at creating 'a people, a name, a praise, and a glory.'[12] Now he will have this. He *alone* will be exalted in that day. When all the ransomed church of God is saved to sin no more,[13] their testimony will be, 'Not to us, O Lord, not to us, but to your name give glory; for the sake of your steadfast love and your faithfulness.'[14] He will be *loved and lauded, extolled and enjoyed, admired and adored, savored and served* as the superior, splendid, sovereign, significant, and satisfying Person He is. Each of the redeemed will join Mary and say: 'My soul magnifies the Lord, and my spirit rejoices in God my Savior ... for he who is mighty has done great

10. Ephesians 2:7; Revelation 15:2-4; Revelation 19:9-8.

11. Romans 9:23.

12. Jeremiah 13:11.

13. William Cowper, 'There is a Fountain Filled with Blood', Stanza 3.

14. Psalm 115:1.

things for me, and holy is his name.'[15] We will *revel in Him as we regale one another* with His exploits in our individual lives, saying with the Psalmist, 'Come and hear, all you who fear God, and I will tell what he has done for my soul.'[16] This devotion to Him and delight in Him will be *passionate*. We will 'bless the Lord' with 'all that is within' us.[17] And it will be *permanent*. John shows us the travel brochure for the glorious place of excellence, ecstasies, and enjoyment to which we're headed: 'No longer will there be anything accursed, but the throne of God and of the Lamb will be in it, and his servants will worship him. They will see his face, and his name will be on their foreheads. And night will be no more. They will need no light of lamp or sun, for the Lord God will be their light, and they will reign forever and ever.'[18]' Best of all, Zephaniah's astonishing words describing the Triune God's pleasure in His redeemed will be fulfilled: 'The Lord your God is in your midst ... he will rejoice over you with gladness; he will quiet you by his love; he will exult over you with loud singing.'[19] In these ways, and no doubt many more, God will exalt Himself forever with an exaltation He secured by humbling Himself to exalt you. Even so, come quickly Lord Jesus!

Christian, this fairy tale ending awaits you. But it's no fairy tale. It's God's Grace Plan for you. You will live

---

15. Luke 1:46, 49.

16. Psalms 66:16.

17. Psalms 103:1.

18. Revelation 22:3-5.

19. Zephaniah 3:17.

happily ever after. When you do, you will know as never before,

THIS IS GRACE.

Doesn't this give you reason to be optimistic about God?

9

The Grace Position
The *Third* Reason Grace Gives You To Be Optimistic About God

'What is "this grace wherein we stand"? ... . (Paul) means our state of justification. It is something that we enter into. We should always think of it as a state or a condition, and it is one in which we derive and receive all the benefits that are attached to this particular state ... God looks upon us favourably and He not only accepts us, He delights to receive us, and He delights to bless us ... We must realize that, being in this position of grace in Christ, we are safe. The final perseverance of the saints is guaranteed by their relationship to the Lord Jesus Christ. The Apostle does not use his words haphazardly, he does not use terms like this incidentally. He and the other New Testament writers agree in saying that we stand in grace firmly fixed, firmly established, secure. It is because we are

not looking at ourselves and have no righteousness of
our own. It is because it is all "in Christ".

Dr. D. Martyn. Lloyd-Jones[1]

WHAT HATH GOD WROUGHT?

Your Grace Position gives you the third reason you have
to be optimistic about God. Your grace *position* is your
unchangeable status before God. It's your *grace* position
because God secured it for you. You may say of it what
Samuel Morse said in the first telegraph: 'What hath
God wrought?'[2] We can put this truth like this: Your
Grace Position gives you reason to be optimistic about
God because it assures you *God continues accepting you
because of Jesus' righteousness, even when you do unacceptable things.*[3]

I. What must you have for God to *accept* you? The Bible's
mindblowing answer is – *RIGHTEOUSNESS!* The head's
side of righteousness is *perfect obedience.* I once preached
this fact to an attentive congregation. I told them that for
God to accept them they needed – from the moment of

---

1. D. Martyn. Lloyd-Jones, *Romans: Assurance*, (Grand Rapids, Michigan:
Zondervan Publishing House, 1972), pp. 32, 33, 41.

2. Joshua Wolf Shenk, *Lincoln's Melancholy*, (New York: Mariner Books,
2006), p. 71.

3. 'Grace' is normally God's free and unmerited favour (sic), his undeserved,
unsolicited and unconditional love. But here (= Romans 5:2, CLC) it is not
so much his quality of graciousness as the 'sphere of God's grace' (NEB),
our privileged position of acceptance by him. ... Our relationship with God,
into which justification has brought us, is not sporadic but continuous, not
precarious but secure. We do not fall in and out of grace like courtiers who may
find themselves in and out of favour (sic) with their sovereign, or politicians
with the public. No, we stand in it, for that is the nature of grace. Nothing
can separate us from God's love.' John R. W. Stott, *Romans*, (Downers Grove,
Illinois: InterVarsity Press, 1994), pp. 141-142.

their birth to the moment of their death, every second of every minute of every hour of every day of every week of every month of every year – perfect obedience in all their thinking, speaking, and acting. From a back pew someone sighed 'phewwwww.' His pneumatic lamentation was right. God's requirement is daunting. But it is His requirement. His lightning flashes from the dark cloud of Paul's 'Cursed be everyone who does not abide by all things written in the Book of the Law, and do them.'[4] You need perfection if you want God to accept you.

The tail's side of righteousness is *your sin's penalty must be paid*. Heaven's bank cancels no unpaid debts. It writes none off. It allows no Chapter 11 bankruptcy to get the justice creditor off your back. 'The wages of sin is death.'[5] Your debt must be paid for God to accept you.

Putting together the head's and tail's side of righteousness comes to this: for God to accept you, you need a *life you cannot live* and a *death you cannot die*. Only God can achieve what you need. And He has. God achieves His righteous requirement for you through Jesus' righteousness. 'For as by the one man's disobedience the many were made sinners, so by the one man's obedience the many will be made righteous.'[6]

II. Six wonderful words describe how God gains for you, and gives to you, righteousness through Jesus.

---

4. Galatians 3:10.

5. Romans 6:23.

6. Romans 5:19.

1. Word one describing how God gains for you, and gives to you, righteousness through Jesus is *substitution*. Abraham is about to slay Isaac at God's command. A restraining order demand stops him. 'Do not lay your hand on the boy or do anything to him.' He looks up and sees a ram caught by its horns in a thicket. He takes the ram and offers 'it up as a burnt offering instead of his son.'[7] 'Instead of' means in the place of; in the place of means substitution; and substitution is the heart of God's gift through Jesus. Jesus is your substitute. Jesus did what He did for you. Jesus lived for you. Jesus died for you. That's what the Bible means by the phrase 'for your sake' and 'for us': 'For you know the grace of our Lord Jesus Christ, that though he was rich, yet *for your sake* he became poor, so that you by his poverty might become rich ... Christ redeemed us from the curse of the law by becoming a curse *for us*.'[8]

2. Word two describing how God gains for you, and gives to you, righteousness through Jesus is *perfection*. Jesus says, 'I always do the things that are pleasing to (God).'[9] From the moment of His conception to the moment of His death – every second of every minute of every hour of every day of every week of every month of every year – Jesus obeyed God perfectly in thinking, speaking, and doing. You can put on a white glove and rub it across even the backroom furniture in Jesus' character without finding the slightest trace of dust. God has done that and holds up

---

7. Genesis 22:12, 13.

8. 2 Corinthians 8:9; Galatians 3:13. Emphasis added.

9. John 8:29.

His glove by saying, 'This is my beloved Son with whom I am well pleased.'[10] Jesus lived for you the perfect life you couldn't live.

3. Word three describing how God gains for you, and gives to you, righteousness through Jesus is *propitiation*. An inmate in the Brazilian prison Humaita teaches you the meaning of this word. He is escorting Chuck Colson on a tour of the facility run by Christians on Christian principles. Colson finds the men joyful, the premises clean, the walls covered with biblical graffiti. The 75 per cent recidivism rate of worldwide prisons is an astonishing 4 per cent here. How is this possible? Colson gets the answer when his guide brings him to the prison's worst cell. This is where notorious prisoners were tortured in pre-Christian days. The guide slides his key into the lock… pauses… asks Colson, 'Sure you want to go in?' Chuck answers, 'Yea. I've seen isolation cells all over the world.' The man turns the key… pushes open the heavy door… and Colson sees him. The cell's lone occupant: a figure of Jesus, hanging on an inmate carved crucifix. The guide says, 'He's doing time for the rest of us.'[11] *That's propitiation!* That's what the Bible is telling you when it tells you Jesus was 'a propitiation by his blood.'[12] Jesus paid your sins' penalty. Jesus did your time.

4. Word four describing how God gains for you, and gives to you, righteousness through Jesus is *justification*. This word conjures up a judge, defendant, and verdict. God

---

10. Matthew 17:5.

11. Chuck Colson, *Chuck Colson Speaks*, (Uhrichsville, Ohio: Promise Press, 2000), pp. 21-23.

12. Romans 3:25.

is the judge; you're the defendant; justification is the verdict. Justification is God's declaration that you have the perfect obedience and punitive suffering He requires. You are 'justified by his grace as a gift, through the redemption that is in Christ Jesus, whom God put forward as a propitiation by his blood.'[13] You are righteous in God's sight with the righteousness of Jesus.

5. Word five describing how God gains for you, and gives to you, righteousness through Jesus is *imputation*. Here's a simple illustration. It's two weeks before your son goes to college. You go to the bank and open an account in his name with a $1,500 deposit. The money isn't his originally. It's yours. But now that it's in his account it *is* his. God did something similar for you the split second you trusted Jesus. He took Jesus' righteousness – Jesus' perfect obedience and punitive suffering – and placed it in your account. Now it's yours. Modern translations of the Bible use the word 'counted' when speaking of this instantaneous deposit but the idea is imputation (= placed in your account and treated as yours): 'For what does the Scripture say? Abraham believed God and it was counted to him as righteousness.... And to the one who does not work but believes in him who justifies the ungodly, his faith is counted as righteousness.'[14] God declares you just because you *are* through the imputation of Jesus' righteousness.

---

13. Romans 3:24-25.

14. Romans 4:3-5.

6. Word six describing how God gains for you, and gives to you, righteousness through Jesus is *incarnation*. The stress here is on the fact it is *God* who achieved this righteousness for you. The One who went from riches to rags by coming into this world to live the life you couldn't live and die the death you couldn't die is none other than the second Person of the Trinity, very God of very God. 'In the beginning was the Word and the Word was with God and the Word was God … and the Word became flesh.'[15] What Jesus has done for you, *God* has done for you.

III. What status does Jesus' righteousness give you with God? This: *God accepts you fully and finally*. Stand before each italicized word as a fatigued man stands under a hot shower; allow each drop to refresh and invigorate. *God accepts* you. The One who made you, sustains you, and to whom you must give an account, is 'for you.'[16] The howling storm of His wrath is replaced by the sunshine warmth of His favor. His attitude toward you is positive. His actions with you are positive. Not some of the time; all of the time. He is for you every day, all day long. Even death won't part you from His favor. Goodness and mercy will follow you all the days of your life, and you will dwell in the house of the Lord forever.[17]

God accepts you *fully and finally*. He doesn't accept you *conditionally*, signing a pre-nuptial agreement letting Him off the hook if you fail. He doesn't accept you *contractually*,

---

15. John 1:1, 14.

16. Romans 8:31.

17. Psalms 23:6.

like a FIFA team signing a soccer player to a contract requiring annual renewal. He accepts you *unreservedly*, as completely as heaven accepted Jesus at His homecoming. He accepts you *realistically*, you as you are – warts and all – without strings. He accepts you *knowledgeably*, with all the skeletons in the closet of your past and the Peter-like failings coming in the future. He accepts you *continuously*, accepting you even when you do something unacceptable. 'There is therefore now no condemnation for those who are in Christ Jesus.'[18] He accepts you unreservedly, realistically, knowledgeably, and continuously because His acceptance of you isn't based on your fluctuating performance but the finished performance of Jesus, now placed to your account. Since Jesus' finished performance is *always* in your account, you are *always* accepted by God.

IV. *Understanding your continuing acceptance by God through Jesus' finished performance is crucial to grace-governed living.* It's your shield when Satan hurls fiery dart reminders of your sinfulness. And he'll remind you again and again. The Bible doesn't call him the accuser of the brethren for nothing![19]

---

18. Romans 8:1. This is 'our position as Christians. ... It is entire, it is complete, it is absolute. In other words, Paul is saying that a Christian is a person who has been taken entirely outside the realm of any possible or conceivable condemnation. The Christian has finished with the realm of condemnation; he has been taken right out of it; he has nothing more to do with it. There is no condemnation to the Christian 'now' and never can be! Had you realized that? Not only is the Christian not in a state of condemnation now, he never can be; it is impossible.' D. Martyn Lloyd-Jones, *Romans: The Law: Its Functions and Limits*, (Grand Rapids, Michigan: Zondervan Publishing House, 1974), p. 271.

19. Revelation 12:10.

Sometimes Satan will try to make you despondent because of some *past* sin. Every sin you've committed in the past has been drowned in the sea of forgiveness as Pharaoh's charioteers in the Red Sea. Yet Satan will seek to give certain sins a Christian burial. He'll resurrect them. He'll seek to haunt you with them. He'll demand, 'How dare you think you're a Christian with *this vile thing* in your past?' You must see what he is doing. He is trying to make you believe your acceptance by God is based on your performance. It's not. It's based on the finished performance of Jesus. Lift up the shield of your acceptance through Jesus and Satan's fiery darts will be quenched like a match in a Hurricane.

Sometimes Satan will try to make you despondent because of some *present* sin. Like an ambulance-chasing lawyer, Satan loves it when you have a head-on collision with failure. He'll try to infect your wounds with doubt. He'll demand 'How dare you think you're a Christian after doing the vile thing you've done?' A pastor in just such a situation models how to resist the devil when this happens.

It's a Saturday and this pastor is at his computer working on Sunday's sermon. Disaster strikes when he knocks a cup of coffee onto the keyboard. The machine drowns. His technical skills can't CPR it back to life. The sermon is gone. The brother shouts 'Nooooooooooooo,' picks up his chair and slams it down. Satan jumps him on the spot, beating him with the brass-knuckled fists of how bad a sin anger is and malevolently asking how he thinks God could possibly use tomorrow someone failing so miserably today. The man of God lies there, about to flat-line, a casualty of a sense of rejection by God. Then the paramedics come in the form of his wife. She stabilizes him by tying a grace tourniquet around his wound. She reminds him the basis of his acceptance isn't his performance; it's Jesus' performance. And because Jesus has performed perfectly, God accepts him even though he has done something so unacceptable as throw a temper tantrum. The pastor lifts the shield his wife gives him and quenches Satan's fiery darts. He confesses; praises God that Jesus' sinless life and atoning death are his; returns to his study knowing God will help him redo his sermon today and preach it tomorrow. The Lord does.

You must do the same anytime you fail. Refuse to listen to Satan telling you God's acceptance is based on your performance. Drive into his heart the sharp two-edged sword truth that your acceptance is based on Jesus' performance. Because of Jesus' performance, God accepts you even when you do something unacceptable. Confess your sin, receive God's pardon, and get up and start living for Him again.

This is your grace position. God accepts you in spite of yesterday's sins. God accepts you in spite of today's sins. God accepts you in spite of tomorrow's sins. God accepts you through the righteousness of Jesus. God gained that righteousness for you and gave it to you. You'll spend eternity enjoying the benefits of this God-achieved righteousness, asking in adoring wonder, with the elect angels and all the redeemed, *What Hath God Wrought?*

Doesn't this give you reason to be optimistic about God?

10

The Grace Privilege
The *Fourth* Reason Grace Gives You To Be Optimistic About God

'You sum up the whole of the New Testament in a single phrase, if you speak of it as a revelation of the Fatherhood of the holy Creator. In the same way, you sum up the whole of the New Testament religion if you describe it as the knowledge of God as one's holy Father. If you want to judge how well a person understands Christianity, find out how much he makes of being God's child, and having God as his Father. If this is not the thought that prompts and controls his worship and prayers and his whole outlook on life, it means that he does not understand Christianity very well at all. For everything Christ taught, everything that makes the New Testament new, and better than the Old, everything that is distinctively Christian as opposed to merely Jewish, is summed up in the knowledge of the Fatherhood of God. "'Father" is the Christian name for God.'

J. I. Packer[1]

---

1. J. I. Packer, *Knowing God* (Downers Grove, Illinois: InterVarsity Press, 1973), p. 201.

God's Christian Name

To live as a Grace-Focused Optimist you must see yourself the way God sees you. God doesn't see you as a 'miserable sinner.' You remain a sinner and your sin is misery-deserving and misery-causing. But you never find Jesus addressing His disciples this way; nor do you ever find Paul beginning a single epistle with 'Paul, an apostle, to the miserable sinners in Corinth or Ephesus or Thessalonica.' Should your identity come from negative language God *never* uses when addressing His children? Just a question I think worth considering …

Another way of identifying yourself that you don't find in the Bible is 'I'm just a sinner saved by grace.' Again, the Bible doesn't disagree that you're a sinner. It won't raise its eyebrows at the notion you're saved by grace. But, like an editor who runs across a plagiarized paragraph in a reporter's article, it has a big problem with the 'just'. The Bible tells you that you're not 'just' a sinner saved by grace. Again, should your identity come from limiting language God *never* uses when speaking about you? Just a question I think worth considering …

According to the Bible, your core identity is the fact you're God's child. God adopting you is THE Grace Privilege. As Saul towered above other Israelites, this privilege towers over everything else God does for you. It towers over everything in God's mind. His fatherhood governs all His dealings with you. It should tower over everything in your mind. You're to be controlled by the fact that you're God's son or daughter. You're not chiefly a miserable sinner. You're not just a sinner saved by grace. You're God's child.

The New Testament makes clear that "Father" is the Christian name for God.'² This means that *God makes a big deal of being your Father and wants you to make a big deal of being his child.*³ This grace truth gives you the fourth reason you have to be optimistic about God.

You find God emphasizing His Father-child relationship with you, and urging you to emphasize it with Him, in five crucial areas of Christian living.

I. Crucial area one where God makes a big deal of being your Father and wants you to make a big deal of being His child is the area of pleasing Him. Here's the way the Bible puts it: *your pleasing God is fueled by your passion for God; your passion for God is fueled by His passion for you; and His passion for you comes to its highest expression in making you His child.* Allow me to cut this into bite-sized pieces.

As a Christian, your heart echoes Paul's words: 'We make it our aim to please God.'⁴ You dread your Lord's frown. You delight in His smile.⁵ I know, I know: the

<hr/>

2. J. I. Packer, *Knowing God*, p. 201.

3. J. I. Packer writes, 'Now, just as knowledge of his unique Sonship controlled Jesus' living of his own life on earth, so he insists that knowledge of our adoptive sonship must *control* our lives too. This comes out in his teaching again and again, but nowhere more clearly than in his Sermon on the Mount. Often called the charter of God's kingdom, this sermon could equally well be described as the royal family code, for the thought of the disciple's sonship to God is basic to all the main issues of Christian obedience with which the sermon deals.' Packer, *Knowing God*, p. 210.

4. 2 Corinthians 5:9.

5. John Calvin writes, 'True piety does not consist in a fear which willing indeed flees God's judgment, but since it cannot escape is terrified. True piety

intensity of this aim waxes and wanes. Sometimes it's active as a three-year old; sometimes it barely has a pulse. Sometimes it runs like a Kentucky Derby thoroughbred; sometimes it's mule slow. But it's always there isn't it? You want to please God.

Your zeal to please God runs on one fuel. That fuel is *passion for Him*. You must be passionate about God in order to live for Him. When Jesus asks Peter, 'Do you love me?' he gets to the heart of what causes you to live for something. When you love something – when you're passionate about it – you'll live for it. A New York City fireman said, 'We're the ones going in when everyone else is coming out.' That's love. It goes in where fear and obligation won't. Love is able to do exceeding abundantly beyond all that anything else can when it comes to living for God. Love God and you'll live for Him. Love God and you'll want to please Him.

Your passion for God is fueled by His passion for you. The drive for your loving God is His loving you. He wants your love and courts it like a man wooing a beautiful woman he wants to marry. How? 'We love because he first loved us.'[6] God loves us into loving Him. If you want to grow in love for God, grow in appreciating His love for you.

Where do you see how passionate about you God is? *God says you see it best in His adopting you.* 'Behold what manner of love the Father hath bestowed upon us, that we

---

consists rather in a sincere feeling which loves God as Father as much as it fears and reverences Him as Lord, embraces His righteousness, and dreads offending Him worse than death.' Ford Lewis Battles, *Interpreting John Calvin*, (Grand Rapids, Michigan: Baker Books, 1996), p. 289.

6. 1 John 4:19.

should be called children of God; and that is what we are!'[7] The phrase 'what manner of' ought to ring a bell. It puts you in a storm-assaulted boat, trembling with Jesus' frightened disciples. While they're quaking, Jesus is slumbering in a coma-like sleep. He is so far under, the alarm clock of the storm's fury doesn't wake Him. The disciples do that, shaking Him conscious with hysterical words about drowning. Jesus rises and speaks a restraining word to the storm, making it cease and desist. The sea instantly becomes calmer than a Norman Rockwell painting. The disciples marvel. Then one voices what they're all thinking: 'What manner of man is this, that even the winds and sea obey him.'[8]

I went to school with a country boy who introduced me to an overall clad word I'd never heard: *onliest*. It was his synonym for something unique. It's the best word I know to answer the disciples' question. What manner of man is Jesus? He is the onliest of His kind. Jesus is *Sui Generis*. Jesus is peerless.

When John says, 'Behold, what manner of love the Father has bestowed on us that we should be called children of God' he is talking onliest. What Jesus is among people, your adoption is with God's love. As He is in a class by himself, it's in a class by itself. God is telling you, 'If you want to know how much I love you make much of the fact I've made you my child. I have no better, richer, sweeter way of showing my passion for you than this. I love you so much

---

7. This translation is the author's combination of the KJV with the NIV translation of 1 John 3:1.

8. Matthew 8:23-27 (KJV).

I've adopted you. And all my dealings with you – ALL of them – are Father-child governed and displaying.'[9] Making you His child is God showing you onliest love!

Christian, if you wish to live a God-pleasing life you must be passionate about Him. If you wish to be passionate about Him you must appreciate how passionate He is about you. If you wish to appreciate how passionate He is

---

9. Puritan Thomas Boston writes of the relation God creates in adoption, 'It is a high and honourable one, John 1:12. As low as we naturally are, adopting grace raiseth us to the highest pitch of honour we are capable of; to be brethren of angels, yea, of Christ, and the children of God. "Seemeth it a small thing to you to be son-in-law to the king?" saith David; but how much more to be the sons and daughters of the King of heaven' Thomas Boston, *Commentary on the Shorter Catechism, Volume 1* (Edmonton, AB Canada: Still Waters Revival Books, 1993 reprint), p. 626. Martyn Lloyd-Jones describes the truth of adoption as 'so staggering and so overwhelming that we find it almost impossible to accept it.' He then rises to the following heights of sanctified eloquence as he expounds 1 John 3:1: 'But lastly, there is the marvel of it all. "Behold, what manner of love!" Words, of course, become meaningless at this point; there is nothing to do but to gaze upon it and to wonder at it all, to stand in amazement and in astonishment. Oh, the quality of this love! Just realize what it means, the freeness of it all, that you and I, should be called and become children of God! The freeness of this love has looked upon us in spite of our recalcitrance, in spite of our unworthiness, in spite of our foulness as a result of the Fall and our own actions. Oh, the love that has not merely forgiven us but has given itself to us, that has entered into us and shared its own nature with us; stand in awe at the greatness of it all! Think of what it cost Him, our Lord Jesus Christ, to come into the world, to live in the world, suffering its treatment, staggering up to Golgotha with that cross upon His shoulders and being nailed to the tree. Think of Him dying, suffering the agony and the shame of it all in order that you and I might become the children of God. "Behold, what manner of love"—you cannot understand it, you cannot explain it. The only thing we can say is that it is the eternal love, it is the love of God and is self-generated, produced by nothing but itself, so that in spite of us and all that is true of us He came and died and suffered so much. The Son of God became the Son of Man that we, the sons of men, might become the children of God. It is true, we are that; we have been made that. Amazing, incredible, yet true!' D. Martyn Lloyd-Jones, *Children of God* (Wheaton, Illinois: Crossway Books, 1993), pp. 16, 19.

about you, you must see yourself the way He sees Himself and you: He is your Father and you are His child. Cultivate the habit of thinking about and talking to yourself this way. That's what John means by adding 'And that is what we are.' You ARE God's child. *This* is your identity, your definition, the central fact in God's heart in all of His dealings with you. Sin doesn't define you; weakness doesn't define you; adoption defines you.

In the crucial area of God-pleasing living, God makes a big deal of being your Father and wants you to make a big deal of being His child.

II. A second crucial area of Christian living where God makes a big deal of being your Father and wants you to make a big deal of being His child is *prayer*. A famous preacher said, 'Christians ought to pray so much the angels say, "These people are always coming up here for something!"' He is right. You can't survive or thrive without praying. God urges you to pray, commands you to pray, invites you to pray, and gives you incentives for praying. His primary incentive is who He is to you. He is your Father. Jesus tells you to focus on this when you pray: 'When you pray, say "Our Father".'[10] Focusing on God as your Father will make you pray gladly, continuously and expectantly because his Fatherhood assures you He delights in helping you. I have a Christmas tree heart when it comes to my children. I can't do enough for them. I love helping them. Why? I'm their father! So, says Jesus, 'If you, then being evil, know how to give good gifts to your children, how much more

---

10. Matthew 6:9.

will your Father give good things to those who ask him?'[11] Understanding you're talking to your Father will make you a person with influence at the throne of grace.[12]

In the crucial area of praying, God makes a big deal of being your Father and wants you to make a big deal of being His child.

III. A third crucial area of Christian living where God makes a big deal of being your Father and wants you to make a big deal of being His child is with your *problems*. The world was stunned the day Superman became a paraplegic. Christopher Reeve, the proverbial 'tall, dark, and handsome' cinematic Man of Steel, was thrown from a horse on Memorial Day in 1995. He broke his neck and spent the rest of his life coping with paralysis. He writes in his autobiography, 'I think a hero is an ordinary individual who finds strength to persevere and endure in spite of overwhelming obstacles.'[13] The Bible agrees. And the Bible tells you that as a Christian the primary way you find heroic strength to persevere and endure is by focusing on the fact God is your Father. This is the airbag truth protecting you

11. Matthew 7:11.

12. James 5:16b. James B. Addison translates verse 16 'the prayer of a righteous man is very powerful in its operation.' He gives this explanation: 'We know that all strength does come from God; but there is a natural feeling that a righteous man's prayer, like Elijah's prayer … carries a mighty punch.' *The Epistle of James* (Grand Rapids, Michigan: William B. Eerdmans Publishing Company, 1976), p. 210. Since the verse's context emphasizes the influence of a Christian's prayers, I believe Addison's translation is correct. However, even if it isn't, the New Testament makes clear again and again that our prayers do indeed carry a mighty punch. See, for example, Matthew 7:7-11 and Acts 4:23-31.

13. Alex Pattakos, *Prisoners of our Thoughts*, (San Francisco: Berrett-Koehler Publishers, Inc., 2004), p. 42.

in your worst collisions with trouble. Listen: 'And have you forgotten the exhortation that addresses you as sons?: My son, do not regard lightly the discipline of the Lord, nor be weary when reproved by him. For the Lord disciplines the one he loves and chastises every son whom he receives.'[14] The message is clear: see trouble as your Father's discipline; not discipline in the sense of punishment but discipline in the sense of the grueling training an Olympic swimming coach puts his star through so he can win a Gold Medal. Your Father controls what happens to you and uses it to make you more like Jesus. Remembering this Father-child relationship will help you stay faithful in the worst problems you face.

In the crucial area of your problems, God makes a big deal of being your Father and wants you to make a big deal of being His child.

IV. A fourth crucial area where God makes a big deal of being your Father and wants you to make a big deal of being His child is *provision*. C. S. Lewis is correct in saying: 'Our whole being by its very nature is one vast need.'[15] Jesus agrees – then tells us not to worry about our needs. But we do. Worries pester us like telemarketing phone calls. How do you conquer them? By enrolling in Nature Theological Seminary and taking its main course.[16] Jesus tells you to look at the birds of the air. Have you ever seen a father sparrow driving a John Deere tractor or a mother Blue Jay

---

14. Hebrews 12:5-8.

15.http://readingisaiah,wordpress.com/2010/11/26/c-s-lewis-on-god-human-need-and-the-nature-of-faith/

16. Matthew 6:19-34.

planting a vegetable garden? Of course not! But their little ones dine on cuisine that would make a chef jealous. Who feeds them? Your Father. If He feeds birds won't He feed his children? Then look at the lilies. Have you ever seen a momma lily sit down at a Singer sewing machine and make clothes for her little ones? Of course not! But their little ones dress in finery that makes Calvin Klein's best look like rags. Where do they get their *haute couture*? From your Father's closet. If He dresses them, won't He dress his children? The cure to worry is focusing on the fact you're God's child.

In the crucial area of provision of your needs, God makes a big deal of being your Father and wants you to make a big deal of being His child.

V. One last crucial area of Christian living where God makes a big deal of being your Father and wants you to make a big deal of being His child is your *passing*. Dust you are and to dust you shall return. How are you to think of the separation of your soul and body? You're to think of it the way Welsh preacher Dr. Martyn Lloyd-Jones thought of his death. He was so ill on his deathbed he couldn't speak. He communicated by shakily scribbling notes on a pad. Here's one of his final notes to his family: 'Don't pray for my healing; don't try to keep me from the glory!'[17] The glory! That's what your passing is about believer. It's about glory because of where death takes you. Hear your Lord: 'In

---

17. https://www.preaching.com/resources/past-masters-d-martyn-lloyd-jones/

my Father's house are many mansions.'[18] You've been away from home on vacation or business. It's fine for a while. But no matter how glamorous or enjoyable, sooner or later you tire of living out of a suitcase. You want to go home. That's death. It's going to the best of homes because it's going to your Father's house. This means it's going to be with Jesus. No wonder Paul says this is 'gain' and 'far better.'[19] It is.

In the crucial area of Christian living that your passing from this earth is, God makes a big deal of being your Father and wants you to make a big deal of being His child.

J. I. Packer has shaped much of what I've written in this chapter. I'll ask him to help me close: '*Do I as a Christian understand myself? Do I know my real identity? My own real destiny? I am a child of God. God is my Father; heaven is my home; every day is one day nearer* ... *Say it over and over to yourself first thing in the morning, last thing at night, as you wait for the bus, any time when your mind is free, and ask that you may be enabled to live as one who knows it is all utterly and completely true. For this is the Christian's secret of—a happy life?—yes, certainly, but we have something both higher and profounder to say. This is the Christian's secret of a Christian life, and of a God-honoring life, and these are the aspects of the situation that really matter. May this secret become fully yours and fully mine.*'[20]

Our brother is correct. The secret to a God-honoring life is reveling in being God's child. That's why God makes

---

18. John 14:2 (KJV), emphasis added.

19. Philippians 1:21, 23.

20. J. I. Packer, *Knowing God*, (Downers Grove, Illinois: InterVarsity Press, 1973), p. 228.

a big deal of being your Father and wants you to make a big deal of being His child. Your adoption is *THE* Grace Privilege.

Doesn't this give you reason to be optimistic about God?

11

Grace Providence
The *Fifth* Reason Grace Gives You To Be
Optimistic About God

'It is a heart-rending thing to reflect on the sin and misery that prevail in this world. Let us relieve ourselves, in some measure, by this consideration, that God has done all things according to the counsel of his own will. Is the Almighty disappointed in his work of creation? Has Satan prevailed over him because of his strength? Or will any real dishonor attach to God by the rebellion of men and angels? Impossible; away with the accursed thought! These clouds before my eyes are dark and lowering – I cannot penetrate the gloom – I see nothing but confusion and wretchedness. The very glory of this world is vanity; its highest enjoyments are unsatisfying. But though I cannot see through this dreadful darkness, I will look beyond it by the eye of faith. *God reigns; all things must issue in the glory of his name, and the happiness of his people.*'

Alexander Carson[1]

---

1. Alexander Carson, *Confidence in God in Times of Danger: A Study of God's Providence in the Book of Esther* (Virginia: G. A. M. Publications, 1990), p. 94. Emphasis added.

'A firm faith in the universal providence of God is the solution of all earthly troubles.'

B. B. Warfield[2]

'"God is love" is the complete truth about God so far as the Christian is concerned… the statement "God is love' means that his love finds expression in everything that he says and does. The knowledge that this is so for us personally is the supreme comfort for Christians. As believers, we find in the cross of Christ assurance that we, as individuals, are beloved of God; "the Son of God. … loved *me* and gave himself for *me*" (Gal. 2:20). Knowing this, we are able to apply to ourselves the promise that all things work together for good to them that love God and are called according to his purpose (Rom. 8:28). Not just *some* things, note, but *all* things! Every single thing that happens to us expresses God's love to us, and comes to us for the furthering of God's purpose for us. Thus, so far as we are concerned, God is love to us – holy, omnipotent love – at every moment and in every event of every day's life. Even when we cannot see the why and the wherefore of God's dealings, we know that there is love in and behind them, and so we can rejoice always, even when, humanly speaking, things are going wrong. We know that the true story of our life, when known, will prove to be, as the hymn says, "mercy from first to last" – and we are content.'

J. I. Packer[3]

PLAYING BADLY WELL

The greatest golfer ever – Jack Nicklaus – calls it one of his greatest golf lessons ever. He learned it from South African player Bobby Locke. Locke impressed on Nicklaus

---

2. http://www.christiansquoting.org.uk/quotes_by_author_w.htm

3. *Knowing God*, pp. 122-123. Italics in original.

the importance of 'playing badly well.'[4] Even the best golfer has a bad round now and then. His drives fly all over the place, leaving his ball in bad lie after bad lie. His putter gets the 'yips,' making even short putts stressful. When that happens it's important to play badly well – to do everything you can to shoot a decent score. There's a spiritual version of playing badly well. It's knowing how to stay close to God when life becomes a dark alley where you're mugged. Hebrews 12:5-11[5] tells you how to play badly well when this happens. It does this with the truth of Grace Providence. Grace Providence is the fifth reason grace gives you to be optimistic about God. Here's the proposition: *When life hurts, focus on the truth that Grace Providence uses Grace Pains to accomplish the Grace Purpose.*

I. *All your pains are Grace Pains.* 'Pains' here is a catch-all hamper for the bad things that happen to God's people. And bad things do happen don't they? Christianity doesn't give you an unlisted number so the obscene caller of difficulty can't reach you. This passage makes that clear.

---

4. Jack Nicklaus, *My Story*, (New York: Simon and Schuster, 1997), p. 20.

5. '*And have you forgotten the exhortation that addresses you as sons? "My son, do not regard lightly the discipline of the Lord, nor be weary when reproved by him. For the Lord disciplines the one he loves, and chastises every son whom he receives." It is for discipline that you have to endure. God is treating you as sons. For what son is there whom his father does not discipline? If you are left without discipline, in which all have participated, then you are illegitimate children and not sons. Besides this, we have had earthly fathers who disciplined us and we respected them. Shall we not much more be subject to the Father of spirits and live? For they disciplined us for a short time as it seemed best to them, but he disciplines us for our good, that we may share his holiness. For the moment all discipline seems painful rather than pleasant, but later it yields the peaceful fruit of righteousness to those who have been trained by it.*'

Reading it isn't like walking through a park full of happy children on a summer day; it's like walking through an army MASH unit just after battle, with a groaning man on cot after cot. Verse 11 says, 'For the moment all discipline seems *painful* rather than pleasant.' The King James Version correctly translates verse 6 with Drill Sergeant bluntness by using the word 'scourge.'[6] This is a metaphor for pain bordering on unbearable. It's like our description of someone's horrendous experience as going 'through hell on earth.' The person didn't literally go through the torments of the damned. But the pain echoed those agonies. It's the same with 'scourging.' Being scourged, your back flayed by repeated lashing with leather thongs, was excruciating. And cancer or bereavement or divorce or being laid off your job, or having your retirement squandered by an unscrupulous CEO – to mention a few of the thongs on life's whip – feels like a scourging. Yet notice what the writer says about your pains, even the severest. He describes them in verse 10 as 'for your good.' He is telling you that your pains are *Grace Pains*. You can say of them what Joseph said of his afflictions, they are 'meant for (my) good.'[7] The day will come when your testimony echoes the Psalmist's, 'It is good for me that I was afflicted.'[8] Notice, 'for our good' isn't used for *some* of your pains. It's used for *all* of your pains, including your scourgings. Every pain you experience is a species in the grace genus. The foulest tasting medicine

---

6. The word is *mastigoi*. It means 'to beat with a lash.' Geoffrey Bromily, Ed., *A Theological Dictionary of the New Testament Abridged in One Volume* (Grand Rapids: Wm. B. Eerdmans Company, 1985), p. 571.

7. Genesis 50:20.

8. Psalm 119:71.

you're forced to swallow is prescribed so you can get well. The rehab making the cure seem worse than the disease aims at getting you back on your feet, fit as a fiddle. The severest pruning cuts your branches close so you can bear much fruit. The first step in playing badly well is having this conviction settled in your mind and heart. All your pains are Grace Pains. ALL of them; EACH of them!

II. *All your pains are Grace Pains because they come from Grace Providence.* Providence is God's government of your life. And providence is big in your nightmare experiences. The first readers of this letter were being persecuted. Verse 3 makes clear that, like Jesus, they were sheep being mangled by the wolves of human hostility. Other Scriptures make clear Satan is always the Alpha wolf in these attacks.[9] So here you have a case of Satan-orchestrated, human-inflicted agony. Yet notice the headline is all about God: 'My son, do not regard lightly *the discipline of the Lord*, nor be weary *when reproved by him* .... It is for discipline that you have to endure. *God is treating you* as sons.' You can't miss his point can you? Your deepest disappointments, most searing sorrows, and greatest griefs come because God sees fit for them to come. Refuse to sit in the seat of the scoffers. Refuse to reject the plain teaching of Scripture and turn away from the only antibiotic that can keep you from the fever and chills of mishandling your heartaches.

---

9. Job chapters 1 & 2; 2 Corinthians 12:7; Luke 22:31; Ephesians 6:10-12. David's depraved debacle narrated in 2 Samuel 11 and following, makes clear that our own sin is also, sometimes, involved in our miseries. Here, too, the bottom line is the Lord's control of the entire situation.

God's providence governs the bad things that happen to you.

What makes this so encouraging is this: *God's providence over the bad things happening to you is Grace Providence.* Your pains are Grace Pains (for your good) because God's providence is Grace Providence. They're for your good because He is for your good. Hebrews 12 gives you three assurances that God's government of your life's pains is Grace Providence.

First of all, the way this passage *labels* your pains assures you they come from Grace Providence. Your English translation tags the bad things happening to you as 'discipline.' That's an unfortunate attempt to house a whale idea in a fishbowl term. The word used here is *paideia.*[10] *Paideia* means childrearing in its widest, broadest, and most inclusive sense. *Paideia* is everything a good father does to prepare his child to live well. But there's a second problem with the translation 'discipline' and its cohort 'chastisement' (scourging). These words conjure up wrong thoughts about your pains. You read 'discipline' and you think spanking. You read 'chastisement' or 'discipline' and you think punishment. While God *never* punishes His children, He *does* sometimes use corrective pain in dealing with them.[11] But translating

---

10. *Paideia* concerns 'the upbringing and handling of the child.' Geoffrey Bromily, Ed., *A Theological Dictionary of the New Testament Abridged in One Volume* (Grand Rapids: Wm. B. Eerdmans, 1985), p. 596. *Paideia* 'sometimes involves rebuke and punishment … But it also involves the positive teaching and training that loving parents will give their children in a whole range of circumstances, to bring them to maturity.' *The New Bible Commentary* (Downers Grove, Illinois: InterVarsity Press, 1994), p. 1349.

11. Simon Kistemaker's dealing with the question whether God ever punishes His children is full of pastoral wisdom: 'Does God punish His

the word by discipline/ chastisement gives top billing to a bit player, making a star out of someone far down in the credits. All your pains, even the harshest, are God's *paideia*, coming to prepare you for the privileges and responsibilities of spiritual adulthood. This fact that pains are *paideia* assures you the providence allowing them is Grace Providence. And Grace Providence assures you your pains are Grace Pains.

Secondly, the *way God is described* throughout the passage assures you your pains come from Grace Providence. God wears only one hat in this entire section. It's His Fatherhood. His Father-child relationship with you is the black velvet on which the writer places the diamond truths of what God is up to in your pains so you can see their beauty. So, verse 5-6, 'And have you forgotten the exhortation that *addresses you as sons? My son*, do not regard lightly the discipline of the Lord, nor be weary when reproved by him. For the Lord disciplines the one he loves, and chastises *every son* whom he receives'; and, verse 7, 'God is treating you as sons'; and, verse 9, 'Shall we not much more be subject to *the Father of spirits* and live?'. God's

---

children? He does send us trials and hardships designed to strengthen our faith in Him. Adversities are aids to bring us into closer fellowship with God. *But God does not punish us.* He punished the Son of God, especially on Calvary's cross, where He poured out His wrath on Jesus by forsaking Him (Ps. 22:1; Matt. 27:46; Mark 15:34). As sin-bearer, Jesus bore God's wrath for us, so that we who believe Him will never be forsaken by God. God does not punish us, because Jesus received our punishment. *We are disciplined not punished.*' Simon Kistemaker, *Exposition of the Epistle to the Hebrews* (Grand Rapids, Michigan: Wm. B. Eerdmans Publishing Co., 1984), p. 374. Kenneth Wuest agrees: 'The word (= *paideia*/discipline) does not have in it the idea of punishment, but of corrective measures which will eliminate evil in the life and encourage good.' Kenneth Wuest, *Wuest's Word Studies: Hebrews* (Grand Rapids, Michigan: Wm. B. Eerdmans Publishing Co., 1947), p. 217. Emphasis added.

providence allowing the bad things happening to you is His Fatherly government of your life. The fact that your pains come from your Father assures you the providence allowing them is Grace Providence. And Grace Providence assures you your pains are Grace Pains.

Thirdly, *God's attitude in allowing your pains* assures you your pains come from Grace Providence. What siphons your morale in hard times, especially a scourging? One heart attack – sharp question: 'How can God say He loves me and allow this?' Yet listen to the Valentine declaration of verse 7: 'the Lord disciplines *the one he loves*.'[12] Get this now. God's thoughts aren't your thoughts and His ways aren't your ways. You look at your bad times and question His love as if His love for you and bad times are as incompatible as heaven and hell. But God tells you that one of the choicest ways He expresses His love for you is through allowing bad things to come into your life, just as a loving parent expresses his love for his child by subjecting the child to painful surgery to remove impacted wisdom teeth. In fact, verse 8 shoots up a flare, warning that it's the absence not the presence of these kinds of pains that indicates God doesn't love you: 'If you are left without discipline, in which all have participated, then you are illegitimate children and not sons.' Throughout my athletic career, my coaches said: 'The time to worry is when I quit getting after you.' Just so with God. His pains assure you

---

12. Puritan Samuel Bolton writes, 'God has thoughts of love in all He does to His people. The ground of His dealings with us is love (though the occasions may be sin), the manner of His dealings with us is love, and the purpose of His dealings is love.' Jerry Bridges, *Transforming Grace* (Colorado Springs, Colorado: The NAVPRESS, 1991), p. 183.

that you have no reason to question His love because they are His love for you in action. The fact your pains come because your Father loves you assures you the providence allowing them is Grace Providence. They come *because* He loves you. And Grace Providence assures you your pains are Grace Pains.

God's government of your life is the Grace Government of your loving Father. This makes your pains Grace Pains. You may say of each of them, even those that are like a scourging, 'This is *from* my loving Father, *for* my good.'

III. *Your pains are Grace Pains because Grace Providence uses them to promote his Grace Plan.* God's Grace Plan is to give you a fairy tale ending that's no fairy tale by making you perfectly and permanently happy. But the only way He can make you perfectly and permanently happy is by making you perfectly and permanently like His beloved Son Jesus. And every instrument in the Great Physician's Grace Pain O.R. is designed to shape you into Christ-likeness. That's what verses 10 and 11 mean by saying your Father allows your pains so you 'can share his holiness' and enjoy the 'peaceful fruit of righteousness.' These phrases are synonymous with Romans 8:29's 'being conformed to the image of his Son.' Let's think together for a moment about why your becoming like Christ is the prerequisite to you being happy.

The relationship between Christ-likeness and happiness is found in a single fact: *Misery and merriment are character-caused.* Mythology tells you life's miseries come from Pandora's Box. Psychology tells you 'problems in living' are caused by genetics or childhood traumas. But God says sin (character) is the cause of unhappiness. Every earthly sorrow comes from 'the fruit of that forbidden tree, whose mortal taste brought death into the world and all our woe.'[13] It's because we're sinners that unhappiness settles on everything like dust on furniture in an abandoned house and clings to everything like a nervous first grader holding tightly to mother's leg the first day of school.

Sin is the cause of *individual* unhappiness. We inflict misery on each other because each of us is a Seth, 'made after the (fallen) image of Adam'[14] Think of the unhappiness you've caused and experienced through ungodliness, lust, greed, pride, envy, slander, and gossip. Abel dies because of Cain's anger; Abraham's lie exposes Sarah to a king's lasciviousness; Hagar suffers because of Sarah's pride; David's lust wrecks Uriah's home; Herod's paranoia erupts in infanticide; Judas' greed, the Pharisees' envy, and Pilate's cowardice put Jesus on the cross.[15] Do you see the issue in each? Each is *character-caused misery.*

Sin is the cause of *corporate* unhappiness. Take war. It has inflicted incalculable harm on millions. Why are there wars? Listen to James: 'What causes quarrels and what causes fights among you? Is it not this, that your passions are at war within you? You desire and do not have, so you murder. You covet and cannot obtain, so you fight and

---

13. John Milton, www.literaturepage.com/read/paradise-lost-1.html
Even the miseries coming from disease, natural disasters, etc., ultimately come from sin, Romans 8:20-22, Genesis 3:17-19.

14. Genesis 5:3.

15. Genesis 4:8; Genesis 12:13-15; Genesis 16:4-6; 2 Samuel 11, passim; Matthew 2:16-18; Matthew 26:14-16, 27:18, and John 19:8.

quarrel.'[16] Take two warmonger examples, one the most blatant in biblical history, the other the most blatant in secular history. *Pharaoh's* lust for power brings war against God, which brings plagues, which bring misery to Egypt.[17] *Hitler's* idolatrous self-love inflicts the Holocaust on Jews and the nightmare of WWII on the world. Do you see the issue in each? Each is *character-caused misery*.

You see the same *character-caused misery* in believers. What robs us of the abundant life Jesus came to give? The villain behind all the misery in Christ's body – all the misery I cause myself and my brothers and sisters and all the misery they cause me – is character-inflicted. All our unhappiness comes because we don't love the Lord with all our heart and soul and mind and strength and don't love each other as we love ourselves.

The point of this is clear, isn't it? We will have no perfect and permanent happiness until we have perfect and permanent holiness. You must become *exactly* like Jesus in character in order to be *exactly* like Jesus in bliss. This means *the best thing God can do for you is work to make you more and more like Jesus*. Praise His Name, that's His Grace Plan for you. And, praise His Name, that's what He is up to in all the pains He allows to enter your life. Your pains are Grace Pains being used by Grace Providence to promote God's Grace Plan in your life.

IV. There are many things you must do to play badly well during life's heartaches. But the taproot of each of them is a firm belief in Grace Providence. By believing in

---

16. James 4:1-2.
17. Exodus 5-14.

Grace Providence and resting in your Father's love, you will find that while 'for the moment all discipline seems painful rather than pleasant, but later it yields the peaceful fruit of righteousness to those who have been trained by it.'[18] I can assure you the Grace Providence taproot is deep and strong enough to withstand the strongest winds. I'm feeling these winds even as I write. My wife and I lost our best friend this past week. He was a thirteen and a half year old schnauzer named Bud. To say Bud was a member of our family is like saying Elvis Presley was an okay singer. We loved him and he loved us. To say his death broke our hearts is like saying kidney stones are uncomfortable. His leaving ripped our hearts out. Tears scald my cheeks as I think of him now. It feels like a scourging. But Hebrews 12 is helping me to play badly well by helping me to focus on the fact that my pain is a Grace Pain. It's being used by my heavenly Father in His Grace Providence to promote His Grace Plan for me. The same is true for you Christian. ALL your pains are Grace Pains. ALL your pains are governed by Grace Providence. ALL your pains are being used to promote the Grace Plan of making you perfectly and permanently like Jesus so you can be perfectly and permanently happy.

This is the truth of Grace Providence.

Doesn't this give you reason to be optimistic about God?

---

18. Hebrews 12:11.

12

Grace Provision
The *Sixth* Reason Grace Gives You To Be Optimistic About God

'Let us meditate upon the Lord's holy name, that we may trust him the better and rejoice the more readily. He is in character holy, just, true, gracious, faithful and unchanging. Is not such a God to be trusted? He is all-wise, almighty, and everywhere present, can we not cheerfully rely upon him? Yes, we will do so at once, and do so without reserve. Jehovah-Jireh will provide, Jehovah-Shalom will send peace, Jehovah-Tsidekenu will justify, Jehovah-Shammah will be forever near, and in Jehovah-Nissi we will conquer every foe. They that know thy name will trust thee; and they that trust thee will rejoice in thee, O Lord.'

C. H. Spurgeon[1]

---

1. C. H. Spurgeon, *Cheque Book of the Bank of Faith*, (Great Britain: Christian Focus Publications, 1996), p. 130.

The Great Physician Still Makes House Calls

I suffered from ear infections when I was a child. They hurt. Sometimes I had to see a doctor. There's nothing unusual about that. Except for the fact I saw the doctor by the doctor seeing me. Our family doctor – William P. Fey – lived next door. And he made house calls.

Dr. Fey didn't play golf. He played xylophone. He didn't play as much as he wanted. All those house calls you know. I'm sure that's why he was usually grumpy when he came over. Who wants to be playing the eardrum when you could be playing the xylophone? Maybe it's because of patients like me house calling doctors like Bill Fey are T-Rexes. No doctor routinely makes house calls nowadays. Except one. The Great Physician still makes house calls. That's what His help is. And He is always ready to help you. This is the truth of God's Grace Provision. His provision gives you the sixth reason you should be optimistic about Him. The proposition is, *Grace Provision is your heavenly Father's readiness to help you.* Six thoughts from a cluster of passages sum up the truth of Grace Provision.

I. The *kaleidoscope of figures* God uses to describe His relation to you emphasizes He is ready to help you. This is the message of Psalm 23, John 15:1-2, and John 20:17. Each of these verses assures you that – like an emergency room doctor, a lifeguard at the beach, a blue-vested smiling gentleman greeting you at WalMart – the Lord is out to help you. Psalm 23 tells you the Lord is your Shepherd. A shepherd provides for his sheep. As the Lord's sheep you can say, 'I shall not want.' John 15:1-2 tells you the Lord is your Vine. A vine supplies its branches with fruit-producing sap. As the Lord's branch you can say, 'I shall bear much fruit.' John 20:17 tells you the Almighty is your Father. A father looks after his children. As the Lord's child you can say, 'Abba shall give me my daily bread, forgive me my trespasses, lead me not into temptation but deliver me from evil.' Everything God is to you emphasizes He is ready to help you.

II. God's *description of prayer* assures you He's ready to help you. This is the message of Hebrews 4:15-16: 'For we do not have a high priest who is unable to sympathize with our weaknesses, but one who in every respect has been tempted as we are, yet without sin. Let us then with confidence draw near to the throne of grace, that we may receive mercy and find grace to help in time of need.' The King you approach when praying is the Savior who lived for you. He has experienced the same East of Eden difficulties you experience. He has experienced temptation's strongest winds. He has experienced trial's hottest furnace. He has experienced these things successfully. He has experienced them so He can understand and help you. He is now enthroned as Lord over all. There's nothing He can't do. There's no one He can't handle. His life and lordship make His throne a throne of grace. It's a place where you'll receive grace any time you come. You may approach it in the confidence you won't come away empty-handed. The way He talks about prayer assures you He is ready to help you.

III. God's *history of helping you* assures you He is ready to help you. If you've been a Christian for any length of time, your life is a diary of divine deliverances. Your days are a thick scrapbook of the Lord's exploits. Like Israel, you can look back and see the bodies of Egyptian troubles dead on the seashore of your past.[2] Like David, the Lord has delivered you from the paws of lions and bears, and maybe even from the hand of some Philistine.[3] With the Psalmist you can say, 'This poor man cried, and the Lord heard him and saved him out of all his troubles.'[4] Read your diary, Christian! Thumb through your scrapbook. Look at the Lord's history with you. Look at the surgeries and sicknesses and sorrows He has helped you handle. Then allow Professor Paul to teach you the lesson God wants you to learn from your history of His help. 'At my first defense no one came to stand by me, but all deserted me. May it not be charged against them. But the Lord stood by me and strengthened me, so that through me the message might be fully proclaimed and all the Gentiles might hear it. So I was rescued from the lion's mouth.' There, you see, he's reading about a recent history of the Lord's help. And what deduction does he draw? 'The Lord will rescue me from every evil deed and bring me safely into his heavenly kingdom. To him be glory forever and ever.'[5] The logic is elementary, my dear Watson. If God has helped you it demonstrates how willing He is to help you. What He did *then* is your assurance He'll do it *now*. Like Newton says: 'Tis grace hath brought us safe thus far / 'tis grace shall lead us home.' The help He has already given you assures you He is ready to help you.

2. Exodus 14:30.

3. 1 Samuel 17:36-37; 50-51.

4. Psalm 34:6.

5. 2 Timothy 4:16-18.

IV. The way the Lord Jesus *describes the Holy Spirit* assures you He is ready to help you. This is the message of John 14:16: 'And I will ask the Father, and he will give you another Helper, to be with you forever.' The Spirit is with you to help you. Scripture indicates that while He always helps us, His help is especially prominent in crises. When you're in the wilderness confronting temptation, He'll help you.[6] When you're in desperate need and don't know how to pray, He'll help you.[7] When you need boldness to be faithful to Jesus, He'll help you.[8] When you're struggling to produce the fruit of Christ-like character, He'll help you.[9] When you're called to suffer for Jesus' sake, He'll help you.[10] When your situation is at its worst, He'll help you.[11] The presence of the Holy Spirit in your life assures you God is ready to help you.

V. More than anything else, *the cross* assures you God is ready to help you. This is the message of Romans 8:32: 'He who did not spare his own Son but gave him up for us all, how will he not also with him graciously give us all things.' Your greatest need was deliverance from God's wrath. God met that need with His greatest gift: Jesus. God didn't spare Him. When the time came for Jesus to suffer the hurt your sins deserved, the Father didn't lessen the pain. Jesus wasn't sedated senseless. Judgment's fist wasn't

6. Matthew 4:1-11.

7. Romans 8:26-27.

8. Acts 4:31.

9. Galatians 5:22-23.

10. Acts 7:55.

11. 2 Corinthians 12:9-10.

gloved. God's mill ground Him exceedingly fine. God not sparing His Son was His helping you. If He helped you by meeting your greatest need with His greatest gift *while you were His enemy*, can you doubt He'll help you with your lesser needs *now that you're His child*? Paul can't.[12] Neither should you. The cross assures you God will graciously give you all things.

VI. The message of God's metaphors; the Bible's description of prayer; God's history of helping you; Jesus' description of the Holy Spirit; and Jesus' cross all assure you God is ready to help you. Lastly, the Lord assures you that the help He will give you will be *enough*. This is the message of 2 Corinthians 12:9: 'But he said to me, "My grace is sufficient for you, for my power is made perfect in weakness."' You'll find His help enough when He calls you to obey an Abraham command to sacrifice some Isaac.[13] You'll find His help enough when David-like you find yourself in some Ziklag where 'all things seem against you to drive you to despair.'[14] You'll find His help enough when no one stands by you.[15] Best of all, you'll find His help enough when you walk through the valley of the shadow of death.[16]

Because of Grace Provision's assurance God is ready to help you, you will one day say with Jacob, '… God who has

---

12. Romans 5:10.

13. Genesis 22, passim.

14. 1 Samuel 30:1-6.

15. 2 Timothy 4:16-17.

16. Psalm 23:4.

been my shepherd all my life long to this day ... (and) has redeemed me from all evil.'[17]

The Great Physician still makes house calls.

Doesn't this give you reason to be optimistic about God?

---

17. Genesis 48:15-16.

13

Grace Promises
The *Seventh* Reason Grace Gives You To Be Optimistic About God

There is in the Bible 'a perfect wealth of promises, suitable to every kind of experience and every condition of life ... There are "shalls" and "wills" in God's treasury for every condition. About God's infinite mercy and compassion, – about His readiness to receive all who repent and believe, – about His willingness to forgive, pardon, and absolve the chief of sinners, – about His power to change hearts and alter our corrupt nature, – about the encouragements to pray, and hear the gospel, and draw near to the throne of grace, – about strength for duty, comfort in trouble, guidance in perplexity, help in sickness, consolation in death, support under bereavement, happiness beyond the grave, reward in glory, – about all these things there is an abundant supply of promises in the Word. No one can form an idea of its abundance unless he carefully searches the

Scripture, keeping the subject steadily in view. If anyone doubts it, I can only say, 'Come and see.

J. C. Ryle[1]

The Word of a Gentleman of the Most-Strict and Sacred Honor

They found missionary David Livingstone dead, kneeling by his cot in his African hut. His Bible was on the cot, open to his favorite verse, Matthew 28:20. Scribbled next to the verse was, 'The word of a gentleman.' This was a shortened version of what Livingstone had written in his journal. There it was, 'It's the word of a gentleman of the most-strict and sacred honor so there's an end of it!' This was his way of reminding himself he could trust the Lord to keep His promises. A gentleman's word in Livingstone's day was equivalent to an ironclad contract. If a gentleman told you he would do something, he would do it. Jesus told Livingstone, 'I'll always be with you.' Livingstone believed this to be the word of the consummate gentleman, the Lord who keeps all His promises.[2]

The fact the Lord's word is the word of the consummate gentleman brings us to God's Grace Promises. His Grace Promises are the seventh reason grace gives you to be optimistic about God. The proposition is, *God's Grace Promises arm you to live for Him, especially when you find it hard to do so.*

I. *God has made Grace Promises to you.* Peter tells you: 'His divine power has granted to us all things that pertain

---

1. John Piper, *Future Grace*, (Sisters, Oregon: Multnomah Books, 1995), pp. 15-16.

2. Harold J. Sala *Heroes* (Uhrichsville, Ohio: Promise Press, 1998), p. 21.

to life and godliness through the knowledge of him who called us to his own glory and excellence, by which *he has granted to us his precious and very great promises*, so that through them you may become partakers of the divine nature, having escaped from the corruption that is in the world because of sinful desire.'[3] One of the ways God's promises are 'very great' is in number. Estimates of the number of promises in the Bible run from 3,000 to 7,000. While there may be difference of opinion on count, there is none on content. Everyone will tell you that each of these promises assures you of a particular good God has the will and skill to do for you or give to you. Every Grace Promise God makes is a check He writes to you, ready for you to endorse and cash at the bank of His generosity.

II. God *makes a Grace Promise for every situation you face.*[4] Look again at Peter's assurance. He tells you God has 'granted to us *all things that pertain to life and godliness through … his precious and very great promises.*' His grace promises contain everything you need to handle life His way. In His closet you'll find a promise suit or dress for every occasion. In His workshop you'll find a promise tool for every job. On His staff is a promise specialist for every ailment. You never swim in waters unwatched by a lifeguard promise. There are promises for temptation and trial; sickness

---

3. 2 Peter 1:3-4, emphasis added.

4. Charles Simeon writes, God's promises 'are "exceeding great and precious," and comprehend every thing which our necessities require. Place us in any situation that can possibly be imagined, and there will be found a promise directly applicable to our state.' *Expository Outlines on the Whole Bible, Vol. 20* (Grand Rapids, Michigan: Baker Book House, 1988 reprint), p. 287.

and sin; discouragement and death; abounding times and abasing times; ordinary days and extraordinarily difficult days. No matter where you find yourself, God gives you a great and precious assurance of some good He has the will and skill to do you. This is His way of assuring you He ALWAYS has the will and skill to help you!

III. *God makes these Grace Promises to arm you to live for Him, especially when it's hard to do so.* Your Father 'knows our frame, he remembers that we are dust.'[5] He knows how weak you are. He knows how strong Satan and the world are. He knows your flesh, the world, and the devil make living for Him as difficult as sailing against headwinds. It's not easy to obey Him when obedience will be an altar where you sacrifice friends or your career as Moses did.[6] It's not easy to submit to Him when some dream turns into a nightmare for you as it did for Joseph.[7] It's not easy to keep your heart with all diligence when you're standing outside in the courtyard, surrounded by unbelievers, as Peter was.[8] It's not easy humbling yourself before the Lord when some Hanani scripture rebukes you for sin and tells you 'you have done foolishly' as that prophet indicted King Asa.[9] Barracks Christianity is easy. Battlefield Christianity isn't. Your Father knows this. So He arms you with His promises so you can say with David: 'For by you I can run

---

5. Psalm 103:14.

6. Exodus 2:11-15.

7. Genesis 39, passim.

8. Matthew 26:69-75.

9. 2 Chronicles 16:9.

against a troop, and by my God I can leap over a wall.'[10] His promises are ally and armor. They're able to help you defeat any enemy attacking you. So you find Him promising to be always with you, always for you, allowing nothing to separate you from His love.[11] So you find Him promising to forgive you when you fail, hear you when you pray, and strengthen you in your weaknesses.[12] So you find Him promising to give you wisdom when you're puzzled, courage when you're fearful, and peace when you're anxious.[13] So you find Him enthroning over your life a royal promise whose scepter holds sway over all: 'And we know that for those who love God all things work together for good, for those who are called according to his purpose.'[14] He gives you these promises to help you live as Abraham's child, walking in your spiritual father's footsteps: 'No unbelief made him waver concerning the promise of God, but he grew strong in his faith as he gave glory to God, fully convinced that God was able to do what he promised.'[15] Abraham handled life through God's promises. God wants you to do the same. He wants you to use His promises to encourage, cheer, strengthen, calm, and motivate yourself, especially when you find the going tough.

IV. The acronym USE can help you employ God's promises the way He wants you to. It stands for *Understanding,*

---

10. 2 Samuel 22:30.

11. Matthew 28:20, Hebrews 13:5-6; Romans 8:31; Romans 8:37-39.

12. 1 John 1:9; Matthew 7:7-11; 2 Corinthians 12:9.

13. James 1:5; Isaiah 41:10; Philippians 4:6-7.

14. Romans 8:28.

15. Romans 4:20-21.

Searching, and *Embracing.* You USE God's promises, first of all, by *understanding* what He has promised to do for you. Become a promise bloodhound. Pay close attention to the promises you find in your Bible reading. Never speed by a promise; put on the breaks, get out of the car, pause and investigate each promise as Moses did the burning bush. Labor to understand just what God is promising you. Find a way to file each promise so you can find it when you need it.[16] Secondly, in a time of need start *searching* for the specific promise that fits your situation. There is a flat head promise and a Phillips head promise in God's promise toolbox; an aspirin promise for life's headaches and an antacid promise for its upset stomachs in God's promise medicine cabinet. You get the point. There is a specific promise for specific needs. When need arises find it. Ask yourself, 'What has my Father promised to do for me in this situation?' Sometimes a promise will volunteer for service the moment the call goes out. At other times, you'll

---

16. You might want to gather *a handful of basic promises* speaking to typical situations, a promissory First Aid Kit with remedies for life's usual cuts and bruises. My kit has in it God's promises of the Holy Spirit's help (Luke 11:13), wisdom (James 1:5), forgiveness (1 John 1:9), strength in weakness (2 Cor. 12:9-10), strength for weariness (Isa. 40:28-31), and courage to face situations out of my comfort zone (2 Tim. 1:7). I have used these soldier promises in so many battles they deserve to be retired on a full military pension. You might want to enlist your own promise militia. You might also consider having a Jonathan promise strengthening you as he strengthened David (1 Sam. 23:16), a promise you turn to again and again and find it there for you, sturdy, robust, energizing, especially when no other promise comes to mind or seems to fit. 2 Chronicles 16:9 is my Jonathan. Again and again, I bring this promise to my Lord, saying, 'Savior, you tell me you're looking for someone whom you can help. Here am I; help me!' I recommend that you find a Jonathan promise too. Appendix one suggests a number of basic promises as a Promissory First Aid Kit for daily use.

need to muster your promise troops and examine them to see which is best suited for the job. But don't rest until you find the promise that best fits your need. Thirdly, you must *embrace* the promise speaking to your need. Claim it for yourself – not hesitantly like a teenage boy asking a pretty girl for a date but boldly like a man claims money he has deposited in his bank account. Cling to it through thick and thin, telling the Lord Jacob-like that you will not let go until He gives you the blessing promised.[17] Expect God to keep it as surely as your Savior expected His Father to raise Him on the third day. After all, the promise Jesus leaned on came from the same Person who makes promises to you. In each case, the promise is the word of a Gentleman of the most strict and sacred honor so there's the end of it!

Christian, the consummate Gentleman arms you with His promises to help you live for Him, especially when it's hard to do so. He can't break a single promise. And won't.

Doesn't this give you reason to be optimistic about God?

---

17. Genesis 32:26.

14

Grace Power
The *Eighth* Reason Grace Gives You To Be Optimistic About God

'There is no higher priority in the believer's life than to delight himself in the love of Christ.'

Maurice Roberts[1]

'"God is love" is the complete truth about God so far as the Christian is concerned ... the statement "God is love" means that his love finds expression in everything that he says and does. The knowledge that this is so for us personally is the supreme comfort for Christians. As believers, we find in the cross of Christ assurance that we, as individuals, are beloved of God; "the Son of God ... loved *me* and gave himself for *me*" (Gal 2:20). Knowing this, we are able to apply to ourselves the promise that all things work together for good to them that love God and are called according to his purpose (Rom 8:28). Not just

---

1. *Sifted Silver*, p. 172.

some things, note, but *all* things! Every single thing that happens to us expresses God's love to us, and comes to us for the furthering of God's purpose for us. Thus, so far as we are concerned, God is love to us—holy, omnipotent love—at every moment and in every event of every day's life. Even when we cannot see the why and the wherefore of God's dealings, we know that there is love in and behind them, and so we can rejoice always, even when, humanly speaking, things are going wrong. We know that the true story of our life, when known, will prove to be, as the hymn says, "mercy from first to last"—and we are content.'

J. I. Packer[2]

'A man cannot look upon the love of God and of Christ in the gospel, but it will change him to be like God ... When we see the love of God in the gospel, and the love of Christ giving himself for us, this will transform us to love God.'

Richard Sibbes[3]

I Am Conscious of a Clean Power

She was a spirit-medium living in Sandfields, Aberavon, Wales. She led a spiritist meeting every Sunday night. One Sunday she was ill and cancelled the evening's meeting. Something caught her attention as she sat at home that night. She saw a lot of people walking to church. They were obviously eager to get there. Intrigued, she joined them. And found herself under the preaching of Dr. Martyn Lloyd-Jones. She continued coming and became a Christian. Here's what she later told the preacher: 'The moment I entered your chapel and sat down on a seat amongst the

---

2. *Knowing God*, pp. 122-123. Italics in original.

3. http://www.apuritansmind.com/puritan-favorites/puritan-favorites-richard-sibbes-1557-1635

people, I was conscious of a supernatural power. I was conscious of the same sort of supernatural power as I was accustomed to in our spiritist meetings, but there was one big difference; I had a feeling that the power in your chapel was a *clean* power.'[4] The clean power that enabled this woman to become a Christian is available to help you live a Christian life. This is the truth of Grace Power. Grace Power is the eighth reason grace gives you to be optimistic about God. I can put that truth like this: *God empowers you to live for Him by love.* Let's look at God's way of giving you strength to live for Him.

I. *God empowers you to live for Him.* One of my favorite miracles is the Lord healing a lame man through Peter. The congenital cripple sits each day by the Beautiful Gate of the temple begging alms, no doubt because religious people are often soft touches when it comes to humanitarian relief. As Peter and John head into the temple the man holds out his tin cup and asks them to give. Peter stops, gazes at him, and tells him, 'Look at us.' Thinking he has struck charity pay dirt, the man fixes his attention on them. Peter tells him, 'I have no silver and gold, but what I do have I give you. In the name of Jesus Christ of Nazareth, rise up and walk.' Then Peter does something that moves me deeply. He reaches out his hand and helps the man up. 'And he took him by the right hand and raised him up, and immediately his feet and ankles were made strong.'[5] I love the juxtaposition here of command and assistance. It illustrates the encouraging

---

4. Iain H. Murray, *D. M. Lloyd-Jones, The First Forty Years*, (Edinburgh: The Banner of Truth Trust, 1982), p. 221. Emphasis in original.

5. Acts 3:1-8.

truth that when God asks you to do something He will help you do it. His help is always available and supremely sufficient. That's the message of the entire Bible. Here are a few representative verses: 'No temptation has overtaken you that is not common to man. God is faithful, and he will not let you be tempted beyond your ability, but with the temptation he will also provide the way of escape, that you may be able to endure it ... And we all, with unveiled face beholding the glory of the Lord, are being transformed into the same image from one degree of glory to another. For this comes from the Lord who is the Spirit ... I can do all things through him who strengthens me ... (H)e has said, "I will never leave you nor forsake you." So we can confidently say, "The Lord is my helper; I will not fear what man can do to me?"'[6] Each of these verses (and there are many more) assures you the Lord is no Pharaoh demanding brick but not giving straw. He gives you the straw of His help for every brick He asks you to make. He is ready to help you obey every command, defeat every temptation, conquer every trial, and meet every challenge coming your way. You can live for Him because He assures you, 'Fear not, for I am with you; be not dismayed, for I am your God; I will strengthen you, I will help you, I will uphold you with my righteous right hand.'[7]

II. *God empowers you by loving you.*[8] Let the truth that God loves you *individually* – you with all your faults,

---

6. 1 Corinthians 10:13; 2 Corinthians 3:18; Philippians 4:13; Hebrews 13:5-6.

7. Isaiah 41:10.

8. 'Love ... is the great *influential principle of the Gospel.* The religion of Jesus is pre-eminently a religion of motive: it excludes every compulsory principle; it

foolishness, fickleness, faltering, and failing – possess your mind as money does a greedy man's and you WILL live for Him. Let the fact that God loves you *personally* – you with all your willfulness, weakness, and wandering – seize your life as ambition for higher office does a politician's and you WILL dread the thought of displeasing Him and delight in the thought of pleasing Him. Believe God loves *you* – embrace this truth with any sense of appreciation of its wonder – and it WILL cast a gracious spell over you making you say with the hymn writer, 'Were the whole realm of nature mine, / That were a present far too small, / Love so amazing, so divine, / demands my soul, my life,

---

arrays before the mind certain great and powerful motives with which it enlists the understanding, the will, and the affections, in the active service of Christ. Now the law of Christianity is not the law of coercion, but of love. This is the grand lever, the great influential motive, -'the love of Christ constraineth us.' This was the apostle's declaration, and this his governing motive; and the constraining love of Christ is to be the governing motive, the influential principle of every believer. Apart from the constraining influence of Christ's love in the heart, there cannot possibly be a willing, prompt, and holy obedience to his commandments … It is then only where this love is shed abroad in the heart by the Holy Ghost, that we may expect to find the fruit of obedience. Swayed by this Divine principle, the believer labours not *for* life but *from* life; not *for* acceptance but *from* acceptance … Love, flowing from the heart of Jesus into the heart of a poor, believing sinner, expelling selfishness, melting coldness, conquering sinfulness, and drawing that heart up in a simple and unreserved surrender, is, of all principles of action, the most powerful and sanctifying. Under the constraining influence of this principle, how easy becomes every cross for Jesus!—how light every burthen, how pleasant every yoke! Duties become privileges—difficulties vanish—fears are quelled—shame is humbled—delay is rebuked; and, all on flame for Jesus, the pardoned, justified, adopted child exclaims, 'Here Lord, am I, a living sacrifice; thine for time, and thine for eternity!' Octavius Winslow, *Personal Declension and Revival of Religion in the Soul*, (Edinburgh: The Banner of Truth Trust, 1960), pp. 43-44. Emphasis in the original.

my all'[9] – and mean what you say and demonstrate it in your life.

Even though I'm talking about God's love, does it sound as if I'm claiming too much? I'll call a single witness to the stand to vouch for the empowering skill of divine love. He is no ordinary witness. He is the man who lived for God as no one other than Jesus ever has. I call Paul to the stand. He said, 'To me to live is Christ.'[10] Does anyone dare to call this into question? Look at him. Reading about Paul in the New Testament is like bending too close to a hot fire. You're singed with the devotional heat radiating from him. What made him blaze? We aren't left to biographers to tell us. The man himself gives us autobiographical insight into what impelled and compelled him. 'The love of Christ controls' me he writes.[11] By *the love of Christ* he means God's love for him expressed through Jesus.[12] By *controlling* him he means God's love for him ruled his life as dictatorially as a tyrant but with a tyranny that was sweet. Paul's testimony to you is, 'When you look at me – when you see how I savored the Lord and served Him and sacrificed for Him and suffered for Him – and want to know what fueled, fired, and forced me to live as I did, I have but one answer to give. It was God's love for me expressed through the life, death, and resurrection of Jesus Christ that explains me.' The glory for you, Christian, is

---

9. Isaac Watts, 'When I Survey The Wondrous Cross', Stanza 4.

10. Philippians 1:21.

11. 2 Corinthians 5:14.

12. '(W)hen Paul says here, 'The love of Christ,' he means Christ's love to him, not his to Christ.' Alexander Maclaren, *Expositions of Holy Scripture, Vol. 14*, (Grand Rapids, Michigan: Baker Book House, 1974), p. 372.

the fact the same love that impelled Paul, loves you. Paul assures you this is so. 'God shows his love for us in that while we were still sinners, Christ died for us.'[13] Note the pronouns 'us' and 'we.' God loves you as much as He loved Paul. And that love can make you live for God the same way it made Paul live for Him.

III. *How does God bring you into contact with His empowering love?* God brings you into contact with His love by focusing you on His grace. Here is a simple example of this point. God stores His love for you in the battery of His grace towards you. And the cable that connects the battery to your life is focusing on His grace. Let's take a brief look at the battery and the cable.

The battery in which God's empowering love is stored is grace. I give no specific verse here because this is the message of the entire New Testament, as I've sought to show in the Grace Primer. The New Testament is a message of God's love. And it's a message of grace. That's because God's love is revealed through God's Grace. Grace is God's white-hot love for you, amazing in its existence, astounding in its expression, absorbing in its excellence. Grace is God loving you so much He exalts Himself by humbling Himself to exalt you even though you were an unlovely rebel creature deserving His wrath. Grace is God saying to you personally and individually, 'I love you.' God's life-empowering love for you is stored in God's grace towards you.

The cable connecting you to the battery, bringing its power into your life, is focusing on grace. A battery is nothing but

---

13. Romans 5:8.

potential power unless and until a connection is made. God's grace-stored love is of no more value to you than a battery sitting on the shelf at Walmart unless and until you connect to it. And the cable connecting you to God's love is *focusing* on grace. It's as you believe God's grace and talk about God's grace and think about God's grace and revel in God's grace and rely on God's grace and rest in God's grace and take refuge in God's grace and refresh yourself in God's grace that the cable connects to the battery and God's empowering love surges into your life, enabling your engine to crank, the air conditioner to run, and the radio to play. Again, I believe the truths in the Grace Primer teach us God's way of empowering us by His love is by having us focus on His grace. The truths in the Grace Primer are truths the New Testament emphasizes, stresses, tells us to focus on – meaning, they are truths God emphasizes, stresses, tells us to focus on. When you focus on grace you do what God wants you to do. And you find yourself being empowered by God's love for you. I ask you to testify: haven't you been strengthened and encouraged and driven to live for Him by what you've pondered in the Grace Primer? Hasn't focusing on His grace empowered you with His love? Haven't you been aware of a clean power moving in you with Tsunami force as His grace has stressed to you how much He loves you? Having you focus on grace is God's way of empowering you to live for Him.

IV. *What makes God's love so empowering?* I've pondered this. I believe the answer is, God's love for you *makes* you love Him. You don't hear much today about loving God. You certainly don't hear the notion that 'God seeks your love.' But those words caused my first Christian tears. I was reading chapter 5 of Puritan Thomas Watson's book on the Ten Commandments titled 'Love.' I was a young minister, as smitten with Watson as a teenage boy with a pretty cheerleader. He wrote the way Picasso painted, with verve and virility. His sermons were Scripture-soaked, metaphor-rich, and John-the-Baptist-bold – all expressed in bedside manner prose the most compassionate doctor would envy. Thomas Watson was everything I wanted to be so I read him like today's kids read *Harry Potter*. One day his pen carved three sentences into my psyche like a lover using a pocketknife to carve a heart on a tree and his and his gal's initials inside the heart. *'It is nothing but your love that God desires ... God does not need our love ... He does not need our love, and yet he seeks it.'*[14] If Watson had only said God doesn't need my love I'd have stayed Sahara dry. But when he told me God *desires* my love – that there is *nothing* He desires but my love – and that He desires my love so much He *seeks* it – I wept. I think it was the first time I understood what Jesus was saying when He told me the first and great commandment is 'love the Lord your God with all your heart and with all your soul and with all your mind.'[15]

I believe the reason God wants my love is found in *the effect of love*. What happens when you love someone? Love impels and compels you to live for the one you love. Love someone and you'll live for that person. You see a stirring

---

14. Thomas Watson, *The Ten Commandments*, (Edinburgh: The Banner of Truth Trust, 1965), pp. 37-38.

15. Matthew 22:37.

example of love's effect in the story of the dinner at Simon the Pharisee's house.[16] You remember it I'm sure. Simon invites Jesus to dinner. He is a *faux-pas* host. He provides Jesus no social amenities. But a gate-crashing woman treats Jesus as the regal guest He is. She wets His feet with her tears, towel dries them with her hair, kisses them, and anoints them with expensive ointment. What accounts for the contrast between Simon and the woman? Jesus says it's love. Simon doesn't love Jesus. The woman 'loves much.'[17] And her love for Jesus makes her savor and serve Jesus. It's the same with us. Love the Lord and you'll live for the Lord. The Lord knows this. That's why He seeks our love.

'But,' you're thinking, 'Charley, you said earlier that what causes us to live for the Lord is God's love for us. Now you're telling us it's our love for Him. What's up?' This: *it's God's love for us that causes us to love Him.* Go back to Simon's dinner party. Eavesdrop again on Jesus' explanation of *why* this woman loves Him. 'Her sins, which are many, are forgiven – for she loved much.'[18] Jesus' point isn't her love for Him caused Him to forgive her. His point is His forgiving her caused her to love Him. His forgiving her expressed His love for her. And His love for her floods her soul with love for Him. Now, go back to Paul. The love of Christ controls him. Why? Because it leads him to love the Lord. And loving the Lord makes him want to live for the Lord.

---

16. Luke 7:36-50.

17. Luke 7:47.

18. ibid.

This is how God's love empowers you to live for Him. As you focus on grace you focus on God's love for you. As you focus on God's love for you your love for Him is set ablaze. As your love for Him is set ablaze, you live for Him.

Christian, the Lord delights in empowering you to live for Him. He does this by having you focus on grace. When you focus on His grace you focus on His love. And as you focus on His love you find a clean power flowing into your life.

Doesn't this give you reason to be optimistic about God?

15

Grace Perfection
The *Ninth* Reason Grace Gives You To Be Optimistic About God

'It is important to remember that the vision of heaven depicted in the Bible is, in the end, an earthly one. We must disabuse ourselves of notions of clouds and harps and wings, for a more tangible existence, one which bears a striking resemblance to many of the features of life we have already come to know. It is not completely the same, of course. The eradication of sin will have consequences that make it difficult for us to fully imagine what perfection ('new' in *kind* rather than *time* is meant) will be like … The church's final resting place is in fellowship with Jesus Christ on earth—a *new* earth … (This) is the fulfillment of the redemptive purposes of God from the very beginning.'

Derek Thomas[1]

---

1. http://www.fpcjackson.org/resources/'sermons'/Derek'sSERMONSrevelation/revchapt21.htm. Emphasis in original.

'God will one day change our bodies and then he will change this world itself. We expect to see this world that is now full of sin turned into a paradise, a garden of God. In this very place where sin has triumphed…grace will much more abound.'

Charles H. Spurgeon[2]

'We shall live in the body, on this renewed, removed, regenerated earth.'

Dr. D. Martyn Lloyd-Jones[3]

I Have Arranged This and Am Unwilling to Have It Deranged

Charles Spurgeon was listening to one of his pastors' college students preach. The sermon was on the armor of God. The young man mimicked strapping on his spiritual mail with flourish. Clad head to foot, he waved his invisible sword and demanded, 'Now, Satan, where are you?' Whereupon Spurgeon, wily veteran of many a hand-to-hand combat with his infernal majesty, leaned close to the make-believe soldier and whispered, 'Young man, he's in that armor, that's where!'[4] He is in yours too, isn't he?

That would be enough, but there's more. You have a Judas inside of you called 'the flesh' which will sell you out for far less than thirty pieces of silver.

But even this isn't everything. You walk every day, all day long, through a mine-infested field called the 'world.'

---

2. http://www.jri.org.uk/brief/destinyjesus.htm

3. ibid.

4. Stanley Voke, *Personal Revival* (Waynesboro, GA:OM Literature, n.d.), p. 23.

Misstep slightly and you'll end up a shrapnel-crippled casualty.

With so much against you, how can you be sure you'll end up perfectly and permanently like Jesus and, consequently, perfectly and permanently happy? The answer is in the truth of Grace Perfection. Grace Perfection gives you the ninth reason why you should be optimistic about God. Here is that truth: *God commits all that He is to making you all He wants you to be in such a way that, if you don't reach perfection, He will dishonor Himself.*

I. *Your Grace Perfection will take a giant step when you die.* Grace assures you the split second you die you'll experience a majestic metamorphosis. You'll join the 'spirits of the righteous made perfect' in the place the Bible calls 'heaven.'[5] D. L. Moody's testimony will be yours: 'Someday you'll read in the papers that D. L. Moody is dead. Don't you believe a word of it! At that moment I'll be more alive than I am now.'[6] This isn't pious propaganda or a religious shell game. It's reality. Because of Jesus, when you die you'll be more alive than you are now.

The Bible gives tantalizing hints about the glory awaiting you. It tells you that everything making earthly life difficult will be gone, a forgotten nightmare, melting ice before the blowtorch splendor of what you'll be experiencing. You'll be able to say to these kinds of things what Jesus said to the Pharisees: 'Where I am you cannot come.'[7] And if

---

5. Hebrews 12:23, 1 Peter 1:4.

6. http://www.eaee.org/faithhalloffame/dlmoody.htm., 1

7. John 7:34.

God provides you with so much relational, intellectual, emotional, and spiritual good in this fallen world, can you doubt that He will much more do so in heaven's perfect environment by giving you things that will captivate, stimulate, and satiate? If His mercies here are 'new every morning,' can you imagine what every morning in heaven will bring you?[8] Best of all, you'll be with Jesus. That's 'far better' than anything you have here and why 'to die is gain.'[9] Your death will be gain, all gain, and nothing but gain for you. You shouldn't fear it any more than you fear coming downstairs on Christmas Day because every moment in heaven will be better than your best Christmas ever.

II. Sweet as heaven is, it's not your final stop. *The final stop on your grace itinerary is the 'new heaven and new earth.'*[10] That's the Cana marriage feast where you'll drink God's best wine.

Here's a broad outline of the scenario and what it means for you. Jesus will return. When He does He'll usher in the 'consummation,' existence in its final form. He will 'transform your lowly body' so that it will be like His 'glorious body.'[11] He'll also change this present world into His Grace Place, the place where His grace is expressed perfectly and permanently. A modern philanthropic organization calls itself 'Habitat for Humanity.' Jesus will make this earth the habitat for God's new humanity. Like a snake shedding its old skin, it will shed what it once

---

8. Lamentations 3:23.

9. Philippians 1:21-23.

10. 2 Peter 3:13; Revelation 21:1-5.

11. Philippians 3:20-21.

was. All the defacing by sin's vandalism will be removed. Everything from weather to work will be perfected. Lambs and lions will become soul mates. Institutions symbolic of our East of Eden existence will be gone without a trace. Cemeteries, hospitals, police departments, and military bases – to name a few representative examples – will vanish like fog before a hot sun. No Civil Defense siren will ever again fibrillate your heart. Swords will be beaten into plowshares. Wars and rumors of wars will become extinct species. The more excellent way of 1 Corinthians 13 will be everyone's way of living 24/7. Everyone will love in deed and truth. This is the meaning of perfect likeness to Christ.[12] Think of this Christian. You will never again weep as Peter did when the rooster crowed.[13] You will never again lament with Paul, 'For I know that nothing good dwells in me, that is, in my flesh.'[14] You will never again pray with David: 'Purge me with hyssop, and I shall be clean; wash me, and I shall be whiter than snow.'[15] You will never again need to leave your gift at the altar to go and be reconciled to some brother or sister. You will then be 'without spot or wrinkle or any such thing.'[16] Your resurrection body will be as perfect as your spirit.[17] You will never again take a flu shot. You will never again go through the hair loss and nausea of chemotherapy; the agony of open-heart surgery, ventilated assisted breathing, and painful rehabilitation.

---

12. 1 John 3:2.
13. Matthew 26:75.
14. Romans 7:18.
15. Psalms 51:7.
16. Ephesians 5:27.
17. Philippians 3:21.

Stitches, fillings, glasses, and canes and all their ilk will be gone. God's blind Bartimaeuses will all have 20/20 vision.[18] His paraplegic saints run and not grow weary, walk and not faint. His Lazarus people will no longer have dogs licking their sores but will live in the lap of grace luxury.[19] And this perfect happiness will be permanent. Nothing in or about you, in or about others; nothing in or about this earth, will diminish your bliss even for a moment. Everyone and everything will contribute to your happiness as you will contribute to theirs. Best of all, you will enjoy and honor God fully. And you will revel in Him and 'rejoice and exult and give him the glory,'[20] as you spend eternity experiencing the wonder of the meaning of 'God is determined to get glory from you by giving grace to you.' This is Grace Perfection. As the Apostle thought on these things he prayed, 'Amen. Come Lord Jesus.'[21] Doesn't your heart cry the same thing?

III. *God wants you to be sure that you'll experience Grace Perfection.* You will be sure if you understand the meaning of 'If God be for us, who can be against us?'[22] What's God saying to you there? He's saying to you *'Christian, I commit all that I am to making you all I want you to be.'* We've looked in sections I and II at 'all He wants you to be.' We look now at 'commits all that He is.'

---

18. Mark 10:46-52.

19. Luke 16:19-31.

20. Revelation 21:1-4; 22-26; Romans 8:18-25; 2 Thessalonians 1:10-12; Ephesians 1:6, 12, 14; Revelation 19:6-8.

21. Revelation 22:20.

22. Romans 8:31 (KJV).

God committing *all that He is* to making you all He wants you to be means *every Person in the Trinity is committed to bringing you to the new heaven and earth.* The God who is for you is the triune God. Each of the three Persons of the Godhead is on your side. Each wants what is ultimately best for you. Each wants you in the Grace Place of the new heaven and earth, experiencing Grace Perfection.

It's *the Father's purpose* to have you in His Grace Place. He is the one who chose to include you in His Grace Plan.[23] C. S. Lewis was noted for his policy of pushing conversations to their logical conclusions. He called this talking 'to the ruddy end.' Your Father is a 'to the ruddy end' God. Paul is so sure that God's predestination (His choosing you for His Grace Plan) will lead to your glorification (your reaching Grace Perfection in God's Grace Place) that He speaks of your glorification in the past tense as if it's a done deal. 'And those whom he predestined he also called, and those whom he called he also justified, and those whom he justified he also *glorified.*'[24] God the Father's purpose for you assures you that you will reach Grace Perfection in God's Grace Place.

Next, *the work of the God Son* assures you that you will reach God's Grace Place. Jesus didn't rush into the burning building of God's wrath only to leave in its flames some for whom He died. He carried all His chosen out. When He said, 'It is finished,' He meant everything necessary to get you to glory has been secured and will be supplied.[25]

---

23. Ephesians 1:3-4.
24. Romans 8:30. Emphasis added.
25. John 17:24; John 14:1-3.

God the Son's work assures you that you will reach Grace Perfection in God's Grace Place.

Then, *the indwelling of God the Holy Spirit* assures you that you will reach God's Grace Place. The Spirit lives in you.[26] His presence 'seals' you, marking you as God's property as a rancher's brand marks cattle as his.[27] The seal is also the deposit.[28] When my wife and I made an offer on the house we wanted to buy we put down a deposit. We wrote a check for a portion of the sale price indicating we were serious about buying the house. By that check we gave our assurance that we intended to pay the rest of the purchase price. God's Spirit in you – making Himself known by leading you to childlike dependence on your heavenly Father in prayer,[29] and prizing Jesus as the one thing worth everything,[30] and making you increasingly serious about living to please the Lord,[31]- is God's deposit, His way of assuring you the rest is sure to come. God the Spirit's indwelling assures you that you will reach Grace Perfection in God's Grace Place.

If this were everything involved in God's commitment of all that He is to making you all He wants you to be it would be more than enough. It isn't. God's commitment of *all that He is* to making you all He wants you to be means *God devotes every trait in His character to bringing you to*

---

26. Galatians 4:6; 1 Corinthians 6:19.

27. Ephesians 1:13.

28. Ephesians 1:14.

29. Galatians 4:6.

30. 1 Corinthians 12:3; Matthew 13:44; John 6:68; John 14:26.

31. Romans 8:1-11; 1 Thessalonians 4:1.

His Grace Place.[32] The sport of rowing involves unparalleled teamwork. Nine people – eight rowers and one coxswain – sit in a narrow boat that looks like an elongated canoe. Each holds an oar. As the coxswain barks commands, they row together in motivational and muscular harmony, making the boat glide torpedo swift through the water toward the finish line. With no irreverence intended, I believe this pictures what every attribute in God's character is doing for you Christian. Each is a crewmember under the command of coxswain grace, rowing you to glory. God's wisdom, justice, faithfulness, power, mercy, patience, holiness, truth, and love are all being used to bring you to Grace Perfection in God's Grace Place. This fact that the triune God is using every attribute of His majestic Being to bring you to perfect and permanent perfection is what Paul means when he tells you God is for you. And this assures you that, in the words of the old spiritual, you will be in that number when the saints go marching in.

Still, even this isn't everything. God *commits* all that He is to making you all He wants you to be. This is what He is doing in the promise of Romans 8:31. He is going on record, boasting if you will, about what He intends to do for you. Understand what this means. It means *God ties*

---

32. According to Thomas Brooks, God says to His people, 'You shall have as true an interest in all my attributes for your good, as they are mine for my own glory ... My grace, saith God, shall be yours to pardon you, and my power shall be yours to protect you, and my wisdom shall be yours to direct you, and my goodness shall be yours to relieve you, and my mercy shall be yours to supply you, and my glory shall be yours to crown you. This is a comprehensive promise, for God to be our God: it includes all. *Deus meus et Omnia* (God is mine, and everything is mine), said Luther.' J. I. Packer, *Knowing God* (Downers Grove, Illinois: InterVarsity Press, 1973), p. 126.

His reputation to your glorification in such a way that He can't maintain the one without obtaining the other. A story I read years ago explains the point. A pastor visited a dying believer. He asked her if she was sure her soul was safe. She answered, 'Praise God, I am.' The minister pressed the point. On what basis was she sure? She told him, 'God will be the loser if I perish.' The pastor reeled as if slapped in the face. He asked how she dare say that? 'Because,' this sound theologian answered, 'if I perish I'll lose my soul but God'll lose His honor. He has told me if I trust Jesus He'll save me. So, if He doesn't save me He'll dishonor himself. And He won't do that.' Preach it sister, preach it! Don't you see the legitimacy of her argument? Christian, what will be lost along with your soul if you don't attain perfect and permanent happiness? God's reputation, that's what. His good name as the trustworthy God is riding on His keeping His promise to bring you to glory as a believer in Jesus. You can say His reputation is a passenger in the vehicle of your eternal welfare. If your soul has a fatal head-on collision with hell, His reputation dies with it. No air bag will deploy to protect it. No jaws of life will be able to pull it from the twisted wreckage and save it through CPR. If that happens Syrian theology will be proven right. God will be seen as only the God of the hills and not the God of the valleys.[33] The Almighty will be considered a bald Samson-like deity, weakened by the Delilah of some obstacle He couldn't overcome. That's blasphemy you think. Exactly. A blasphemy God will never permit! He will never sully His reputation by beginning a good work in you and not

---

33. 1 Kings 20:23.

finishing it.[34] NEVER. This is why the same Paul who calls himself the 'chief of sinners' can also say, 'For I know whom I have believed, and am persuaded that he is able to keep that which I have committed unto him against that day.'[35] Child of God, you can – and should – say the same!

One of Abraham Lincoln's generals balked at one of the Commander in Chief's orders. Lincoln wrote the man this 'iron sentence': 'I have arranged this, and am very unwilling to have it deranged.'[36] Christian, your heavenly Father has *arranged* for your Grace Perfection. The fact that God commits all that He is to making you all He wants you to be is His way of assuring you *He is very unwilling to have it deranged.* You WILL be perfectly and permanently like Jesus and, consequently, perfectly and permanently happy.

This is the truth of Grace Perfection.

Doesn't this give you reason to be optimistic about God?

---

34. Philippians 1:6.

35. 1 Timothy 1:15 & 2 Timothy 1:12, (KJV).

36. T. Harry Williams, *Lincoln and His Generals* (New York: Alfred A. Knopf, Inc., 1952), pp. 104-105.

Paradigm Shift III

16

Grace Preoccupation
Five Strategies for Staying Optimistic about God

'We do our work largely by the aid of habit ... Many a man who is growing old will every day get through an amount of work that surprises his friends, and it is possible because he works in the lines of lifelong habit. Besides, the only possible way to keep out bad habits is to form good habits. By a necessity of nature, whatever is frequently and at all regularly done becomes a habit. If a man has been the slave of evil habits, and wishes to be permanently free, he must proceed by systematic and persevering effort to establish corresponding good habits ... I think we ought to talk more upon...the power and blessing of good habits.'

John Broadus[1]

---

1. John Broadus, *The Habit of Thankfulness*, http://www.newsforchristians.com/clsr1/broaDUS004.html, 1.

'You can't avoid habitual living, because this is the way God has made you. He gave you the ability to live a life that does not demand conscious thought about every action or response.'

Jay Adams[2]

STRATEGERY

Grace gives you reason to be optimistic about God every day, all day long. This optimism isn't a small matter, the spiritual equivalent of whether you eat eggs or cereal for breakfast. It's crucial to your living a God-pleasing life. To go through a day without it is to be a soldier on the battlefield without his main weapon or a diabetic without her insulin. That's because optimism about God is faith and 'without faith it is impossible to please God.' It's by this optimism that you are made 'strong and do exploits.'[3] So, like the soldier's rifle and the diabetic's medication, you need to keep optimism handy, ready to use at a moment's notice. It would be better to leave home without your American Express Card than your optimism about the Lord. *Staying* optimistic about the Lord has to be your priority, every day, all day long.

You can learn to stay optimistic about God. I know you can because God has blessed you with the ability to form habits.[4] You were born a habit prodigy. You began making habit music at an early age. You've practiced your craft so much you're now an old hand at habit making. And this

---

2. Jay Adams, *The Christian Counselor's Manual* (Grand Rapids, Michigan: Zondervan, 1973), p. 182.

3. Daniel 11:32, (KJV).

4. 'Habit—the capacity to learn to respond unconsciously, automatically and comfortably—is a great blessing of God.' Jay Adams, *More Than Redemption* (Grand Rapids, Michigan: Baker Book House, 1979), p. 161.

skill, this knack, this facility is your best friend when it comes to staying optimistic about God. That's because no one is born with the silver spoon of optimism about Him in their mouths. No one inherits this optimism from a wealthy relative. Every grace optimist is a creature of habit. Since you're a pro at forming habits, you can form the habit of staying optimistic about the Lord.

You need what former President George Bush called a 'strategery' if you're going to develop the habit of staying optimistic about God. You need a strategy, a plan to follow. The plan I offer makes up the *third* Paradigm Shift you must go through to become the Grace-Focused Optimist God wants you to be. I call this shift Grace Preoccupation. You must become so focused on grace, so preoccupied with it, that you eat grace, sleep grace, drink grace, and breathe grace.

The place to start is with understanding that the habit of staying optimistic about God is *a habit composed of other habits*. It's like a pro golfer's habit of hitting good golf shots again and again. The habit of consistently and accurately striking a golf ball is made up of the habits of a proper grip, stance, backswing, downswing, and follow through, together enabling the golfer to swing with a ballerina's rhythmic beauty and hit with the force of a heavyweight boxer's uppercut. Habits of a good swing combine to form the habit of a good strike.

The habit of staying optimistic about God is formed of *five habits of preoccupying yourself with grace*. These are: Engaging in Grace Preaching; Utilizing Grace Polemics; Employing the Grace Pledge; Abounding in Grace Praise; and Practicing Grace Penitence. Develop these habits and they will help you stay optimistic about God every day, all day long.

We turn now to these five habits that make up Paradigm Shift III, Grace Preoccupation.

17

Strategy *One* for Staying Optimistic about God: Engaging in Grace Preaching

'"Think of what you know of God through the gospel," says Paul, "and apply it. Think against your feelings; argue yourself out of the gloom they have spread; unmask the unbelief they have nourished; take yourself in hand, talk to yourself, make yourself look up from your problems to the God of the gospel; let evangelical thinking replace emotional thinking." By this means (so Paul believes) the indwelling Holy Spirit, whose ministry it is to assure us that we are God's beloved children and heirs (vv. 15-16), will lead us to the point where Paul's last triumphant inference— "I am convinced that neither death nor life ... nor anything else in all creation, will be able to separate us from the love of God that is in Christ Jesus our Lord" (vv. 38-39)—will evoke from us the response: "And so am I! Hallelujah!" For in this response, as Paul knows, lies the secret of the "more than conquerors" experience, which is the victory that overcomes the world and the Christian's heaven on earth.'

J. I. Packer on Romans 8[1]

---

1. J. I. Packer, *Knowing God*, p. 260.

I BELIEVE YOU HAVE HEARD ME PREACH

The first strategy for maintaining optimism about God is to Christianize something you already do all the time. You engage in self-talk.[2] You may be constitutionally quiet as a cell phone with a dead battery. You may go all day saying only a few words to others. But like everyone else, there's one person you talk to as often as a teenager talks to her boyfriend. Like David,[3] the Psalmist,[4] and the woman Jesus healed,[5] *you talk to yourself.*

Sometimes your self-talk is in the silent language of thinking. Sometimes it's vocal. Sometimes it's louder than the radio of the teen pulling up next to you at a red light. Sometimes it's quieter than a whisper. Sometimes it's unnoticeable as a subliminal message embedded in a commercial. Sometimes it's rock in your shoe obvious. But whatever form it takes, you carry on a running conversation with yourself. You talk to yourself every day, all day long.

You Christianize your habit of self-talk by training yourself to talk *about grace* every day. Author Jerry Bridges calls this 'preaching the gospel to yourself every day.'[6] But preaching the gospel to yourself means more than reminding yourself that God forgives and accepts you because of Jesus. It means reminding yourself of *everything* you are through

---

2. Shem Helmstetter, *What To Say When You Talk To Yourself* (New York: Grindle Press, 1982), p. 72ff.

3. 1 Samuel 30:6.

4. Psalm 42:5. Martyn Lloyd-Jones says the Psalmist is engaging in what today is called 'self-talk.' *Spiritual Depression: Its Causes and Cure* (William B. Eerdmans Publishing Company, 1965), p. 20-21.

5. Mark 5:28.

6. http://www.sovereigngraceministries.org/blogs/sgm/post/Jerry-Bridges-preaching-the-gospel-to-yourself.aspx

grace. This is the habit of Engaging in Grace Preaching. It's strategy number one for staying optimistic about God. I can put this strategy like this: *To stay optimistic about God, focus on grace by developing the habit of Engaging in Grace Preaching.*

Three questions will help you get a handle on this strategy.

Question One: *What does it mean to preach grace to yourself?* Preaching grace to yourself means telling yourself you are what God says He has made you by grace. It means telling yourself you are what the Grace Paradigm and Grace Primer say you are. It means telling yourself that you are God's child, sheep, bride, and friend. It means telling yourself these things and telling yourself these things and telling yourself these things until you habitually think of yourself as the Grace Person God says you are. The German philosopher Schopenhauer was walking a dark street one night. A policeman stopped him. 'Who are you?' the constable demanded. Schopenhauer lamented, 'I wish to God I knew!' Preaching grace to yourself means telling yourself you are who and what God says you are until your answer to the question, 'Who are you?' is an immediate and confident, 'I am a Grace Person!'

Question Two: *Why is preaching grace to yourself so important?* It's important because what you think about yourself governs the way you live. You may sit as wayside soil in church Sunday after Sunday. The sermons you hear may do you as much good as watering does a plastic plant.

But you're congenial soil for your self-sermons. You hear them and bring forth fruit. Or weeds.

Think about this and you'll see it's true. Preach negatively to yourself and you act negatively. Find a Christian as gloomy as a funeral on a freezing January day or anxious as a guilty defendant waiting for the jury's verdict. Eavesdrop on that Christian's self-preaching. You'll hear nothing but dark, dreary, discouraging sermons.[7] And vice versa. Find a Christian who lives in the sunshine of optimism about God, full of joy and peace and gratitude. Eavesdrop on that

---

7. D. Martyn Lloyd-Jones stresses the connection between what you preach to yourself and how you live. In discussing the 'treatment' for what he calls 'Spiritual Depression' he writes: 'What about the treatment in general? Very briefly at this point, the first thing we have to learn is what the Psalmist learned—we must learn to take ourselves in hand. But he does something which *is more important still … he talks to himself.* This man turns to himself and says, 'Why art thou cast down O my soul, why art thou disquieted within me?' *He is talking to himself, he is addressing himself.* But, says someone, is that not the one thing we should not do since our great trouble is that we spend too much time with ourselves? … . I say that *we must talk to ourselves instead of allowing 'ourselves' to talk to us.* Do you realize what this means? I suggest *that the main trouble in this whole matter of spiritual depression in a sense is this, that we allow our self to talk to us instead of talking to our self.* Am I trying to be deliberately paradoxical? Far from it. This is the very essence of wisdom in this matter. *Have you realized that most of your unhappiness in life is due to the fact that you are listening to yourself instead of talking to yourself?* Take those thoughts that come to you the moment you wake up in the morning. You have not originated them, but they start talking to you, they bring back the problems of yesterday, etc. Somebody is talking. Who is talking to you? Your self is talking to you. Now this man's treatment was this: *instead of allowing this self to talk to him, he starts talking to himself.* 'Why art Thou cast down, O my soul?' he asks. His soul had been depressing him, crushing him. *So he stands up and says, 'Self, listen for a moment, I will speak to you.'* Do you know what I mean? If you do not, you have had but little experience.' Lloyd-Jones, *Spiritual Depression, pp.* 20-21. Emphasis added. Notice that Lloyd-Jones considers our thinking to be a form of self-talk. J. I. Packer describes 'talking to ourselves' as one aspect of what it means to 'meditate': *Hot Tub Religion* (Wheaton, Illinois: Tyndale House Publishers, Inc., 1988), p. 158.

Christian's self-preaching. You'll hear nothing but cheering, consoling, confidence-boosting sermons about grace.

Take Paul as an example of the benefit of preaching grace to yourself. He is the quintessential grace man. He is inexplicable without grace: a Christian Paris without the Eiffel Tower, a spiritual Romeo without Juliet – if you leave grace out of the picture. Paul never does. He sees himself as grace-made, engaging in grace ministry, through grace help, to the praise of the glory of grace.[8] Grace is his Alpha and Omega. Why? He is always preaching grace to himself. You read what he preaches to himself by reading what he preaches to us. His letters echo the sermons he preaches to himself in season and out. 'I can do all things through him who strengthens me ... For I consider that the sufferings of this present time are not worth comparing with the glory that is to be revealed to us ... Christ loved me and gave himself for me ...I am sure of this, that he who began a good work in you will bring it to completion at the day of Jesus Christ ...'[9] Again and again, even when looking at his wretched past,[10] Paul preaches grace to himself.

It's this self-preaching that explains Paul's life. He beats temptation, rejoices in trial, endures extraordinary hardship, and gives thanks in everything because he constantly preaches grace to himself. Grace preaching controls his life.

The same is true for you. You grow what you sow. Begin preaching grace to yourself and you'll begin living

---

8. 1 Corinthians 15:10; Galatians 1:15-16; Acts 20:24; 2 Corinthians 12:9-10; Ephesians 1:3-14.

9. Philippians 4:13; Romans 8:18; Galatians 2:20; Philippians 1:6.

10. 1 Timothy 1:12-17.

a grace-governed life. Preach grace to yourself and you'll find yourself increasingly lost in wonder, love, and praise for the God of grace. Preach grace to yourself and you'll find yourself growing in hatred of displeasing Him and love for pleasing Him. Preach grace to yourself and you'll find your grace sermons bracing you, and encouraging you, and inspiring you, and stirring you to 'expect great things of God and attempt great things for God.' Preach grace to yourself and you'll find yourself getting up quicker when life knocks you down. In sum, preach grace to yourself and you'll begin living as a Grace Person. Sowing by grace preaching leads to growing in grace living.

Question Three: *How do you develop the habit of grace preaching?*

You program yourself. You find a method of preaching grace to yourself and you stick with it until preaching grace to yourself becomes second nature. I share with you now my method as one example of how you might do it. If you like my way, take it – it's yours. If you riff off my riff, fine. If you want to write your own music do so. I simply want to encourage you to program into yourself this habit of grace preaching.

My method of preaching grace to myself every day is through *engaging in Grace Affirmations.* By *Grace* I mean the grace truths found in the Grace Paradigm and Grace Primer. By *Affirmations* I mean declaring these grace truths to myself in some form or fashion every day.

Sometimes I do my Grace Affirmations by *reciting* to myself the truths in the Grace Paradigm and Grace Primer. I wake and before getting out of bed I say, 'I am a

Grace Person. God wants my priority today to be His *Grace Priority* of being governed by grace. He wants me to prize my *Grace Position* of forgiveness and acceptance and my *Grace Privilege* of making much of Him as my Father because He makes much of me as His child. He wants me to enjoy the *Grace Pleasures* He has in store for me today. He wants me to believe He will follow a *Grace Policy* with me today as He continues fulfilling His *Grace Plan* of exalting Himself by humbling Himself to exalt me. Everything that happens today will come from *Grace Providence*. *Grace Provision* will help me handle whatever comes. And *Grace Power* will empower me to live for God as I focus on God's love expressed through His grace. All of this will give me ample reason to offer Him *Grace Praise* throughout the day. One day I will experience *Grace Perfection* as God completes His *Grace Plan*. This is the *Grace Perspective* God wants me to have all day long.' In order to maintain it, he gives me His *Grace Pledge*.[11] Then I ask the Lord to help me live today in the optimism about Him these truths give me.

At other times, I use the Grace Affirmations *as part of my morning prayer*. I work through each affirmation with praise and petition. For example, I pray, 'Lord, I thank you that you have made me a *Grace Person*. Help me live that way today. I bless your Name Father that nothing will happen to me today that isn't controlled by your *Grace Providence* and that whatever it allows your *Grace Provision* will help me handle. Allow this to keep me from grumbling over anything; and allow these truths to keep me peaceful and content.' You get the idea. I have found that praying

---

11. I will explain the Grace Pledge in Chapter 19.

through the Grace Affirmations keeps my praying fresh and creative as I apply it to the day ahead.

Whether by repetition or prayer, I've preached these truths to myself day in and day out for a long time. When I first came up with this idea and began implementing it, I struggled. Sometimes I forgot to affirm these precious grace truths to myself. On more than one occasion I foolishly told myself I was in too much of a hurry to spend time this way and I neglected this sweet helpmate to living a grace-governed life. But I quickly learned that I was more inclined to stay optimistic about God when I preached Grace Affirmations to myself than when I didn't. And I knew I needed to stay optimistic about God if I was going to survive and thrive in the struggle to walk with Him. So I stuck with it. Now the habit is embedded.

I urge you to do something similar. I plead with you to arm yourself with grace before you step on the battlefield. Fill your sling with stones from the grace river before you face your Goliath day. As I say, feel free to use stones from my river or find your own if you'd rather. Either way, find some way to begin your day preaching grace to yourself.[12]

---

12. Here is an example of Grace Affirmation: 'I will live as a Grace-Focused Optimist today because: 1. I am a Grace Person. 2. God has put me in the Grace Position of being accepted by Him because of Jesus even when I do something unacceptable. 3. God makes a big deal of my Grace Privilege of being His child and wants me to make a big deal of it too. 4. Grace Providence assures me that that whatever happens to me today will come from God and for my good. 5. Grace Provision will assist me to handle whatever Grace Providence appoints. 6. As I focus on how much God loves me, Grace Power will empower me to love God and grow in my devotion to Him. 7. Today will take me one step closer to eternity and the Grace Perfection of being perfectly and permanently happy because I'll be perfectly and permanently like Jesus. 8. To maintain this Grace Perspective of optimism about Him, God gives me His Grace Pledge:

Your goal is to become like Samuel Taylor Coleridge. Here is the gist of a conversation Coleridge had with his friend Charles Lamb: Coleridge to Lamb: 'I believe you have heard me preach.' Lamb to Coleridge: 'I've never heard you do anything else!' That's the habit you want Christian. You want to reach the point of never hearing yourself do anything else than preach grace to yourself. Doing that, you will stay focused on grace. When you stay focused on grace you will stay optimistic about God. When you stay optimistic about God you will live the grace-governed life of Grace-Focused Optimism. And when you live the grace-governed life of Grace-Focused Optimism you will honor God, enjoy His goodness, and be useful to Him.

Strategy number one for staying optimistic about God works. Because of this, I recommend that you *engage in Grace Preaching.*

Wherever you are in your story, I will give you grace so you can give me glory. 9. Because God will give me grace all day long I'll have occasion to offer Him Grace Praise all day long. Father, I thank you that you are always up to my good and I look forward to walking through this day with you!' Appendix two offers an 'I Am a Grace-Focused Optimist' set of affirmations as a template for interested readers.

18

Strategy *Two* for Staying Optimistic about God: Utilizing Grace Polemics

'Now we must be careful to observe this rebuke and to understand what He was saying. In the first place, he was rebuking them for being in such a state at all. "Where is your faith?" He says. Matthew puts it, "O ye of little faith!" Here as elsewhere, "He marveled at their unbelief." He rebuked them for being in that state of agitation and terror and alarm while He was with them in the boat. That is the first great lesson we have to apply to ourselves and to one another. It is very wrong for a Christian ever to be in such a condition. I do not care what the circumstances may be, the Christian should never be agitated, the Christian should never be beside himself like this, the Christian should never be at his wit's end, the Christian should never be in a condition in which he has lost control of himself. That is the first lesson ... A Christian should never, like the worldly person, be depressed, agitated, alarmed, frantic, not knowing what to do. It is the typical reaction to trouble of those who are not Christian; that is why it is so wrong to be like that. The Christian is different from other people, the Christian has something which the non-Christian does not possess, and the ideal for the Christian is that which is stated so perfectly by the Apostle Paul in the fourth chapter of Philippians: "I have learned, in whatsoever state I am, therewith to be content ... I can do all things through Christ which strengtheneth me." That is the Christian position; that is what the Christian is meant to be like. The Christian is never meant to be carried away by his feelings, whatever they are—never. That is always wrong in a Christian.'

Dr. Martyn Lloyd-Jones[1]

GET UP, LAD, GET UP!

Chariots of Fire is a movie about two runners: a Scottish Christian named Eric Liddell and a Jewish sprinter named Harold Abrahams. In one of the picture's most dramatic scenes, Abrahams is in France to watch Liddell run. Shortly after the starter's gun fires and the men bolt from their blocks, a competitor elbows Liddell off the track. He rolls like a tumbleweed, stops, and comes up on one knee, looking dazed. The camera pans from Liddell's face to Coach Sam Mussabini, standing in the center of the field, cigar in mouth, stopwatch in hand, muttering something. The crowd noise dims, allowing us to eavesdrop. We hear, 'Get up, lad, get up!' Sure enough, Liddell gets up, gets back on the track, runs as if being chased by a knife-wielding madman, and wins the race.

---

1. D. Martyn Lloyd-Jones, *Spiritual Depression* (Hannibal, Missouri: Granted Ministries Press, 2011), pp. 137-138.

If you're going to stay optimistic about God every day, all day long, you must learn to be your own Sam Mussabini. You must learn to engage in *Grace Polemics*. A polemic argues that one thing is a lie and another thing is the truth. When you get into the pit of discouragement it's because you're telling yourself pessimism-breeding lies. The way to climb out and into the sunshine of optimism is by telling yourself the truth. You do this by arguing with yourself. This is Grace Polemics. It's the second strategy for staying optimistic about God by focusing on grace. It's to be utilized when you've temporarily lost your optimism and need to recover it. I'll put this truth this way: *To recover optimism about God when you've temporarily lost it, develop the habit of refocusing on grace by utilizing Grace Polemics.* David mentors us in Grace Polemics in 1 Samuel 30:6 (kjv): 'But David encouraged himself in the Lord his God.'

I. *Like David, you will sometimes find yourself in discouraging circumstances.* First Samuel 30:1-6 records David's debacle in Ziklag. This Philistine city is a safe house for him and his men while they're hiding from Saul. Now, returning from battle, they find their homes in ashes and their wives and children carried away as POWs by marauders. Grief-stricken, David's men scapegoat him. They become an Old Testament version of a lynch mob by talking of stoning him. David is 'greatly distressed.' All things seem against him to drive him to despair. But if you've been a Christian for any length of time, David's angst comes as no surprise. You know all about Ziklag and its miseries. You may not travel much but your passport has a Ziklagian stamp. Sometimes the flight there takes place in a flash. You get an unexpected medical bill in the mail or your unmarried daughter tells you she's pregnant or the doctor tells you you'll need your third surgery in three years. And you're greatly distressed as pessimism dethrones optimism. At other times, the flight to Ziklag is longer than one from New York to London. You were handling some chronic problem relatively well – maybe it was chemotherapy or caring for an aging and increasingly testy parent or pounding the pavement for six months searching for employment after a bad economy squeezed you out of your job – then, suddenly, you snapped and fell apart, spiraling into great distress as optimism's sun hid behind pessimism's ugly clouds and driving rain. Either way, every Christian visits Ziklag sooner or later. You may be there now. I've got good news for you if you are. You can book a flight out immediately and quickly get back to 'home, sweet home' optimism about God.

II. *You leave Ziklagian pessimism by utilizing Grace Polemics.* That's the travel agent booking David's flight out. 'But David encouraged himself in the Lord his God (KJV).'[2] I think this means that David fought to be optimistic about God in this pessimistic situation. He fought with the sword of a truth-governed explanatory style. Psalm 42:5 models the kind of self-talk your ancient cousin used and God wants you to use too. 'Why are you cast down, O my soul, and why are you in turmoil within me? Hope in God; for I shall again praise him, my salvation and my God.' This

---

2. Some translations read 'But David strengthened himself in the Lord his God.'

verse demonstrates how to use the sharp two-edged sword of Grace Polemics.

1. First, *Grace Polemics begins with challenging the pessimistic thoughts that accompany your hard times.* They come rushing in like soldiers storming a castle. Since David was 'a man with a nature like ours' (James 5:17) he must have found himself on this occasion in hand-to-hand combat with pessimism's fiercest warriors. Doubt, self-pity, and fear must have combined to make him want to wave the white flag of murmuring. No doubt they temporarily got the best of him. But then he fought back. Imagine him using the psalmist's words. He begins with 'Why are you cast down, O my soul.' This is the equivalent of a scolding. David's saying to himself what God said to Elijah in a similar situation. Down and discouraged by Jezebel's threat to kill him, Elijah flees to a cave. The word of the Lord comes to him asking, 'What are you doing here, Elijah?' (1 Kings 19:9). Meaning, 'Elijah you've got no business being in this cave.' 'Why are you cast down' is David saying to himself, 'David, no matter how bad things are you have no business being undone by them.' Christian, you've got to do the same when you're in Ziklag. You've got to fight your negative thoughts. You've got to call thoughts like 'I don't see how God can love me and allow this' and 'I don't see how this can possibly be for my good' exactly what they are – the offspring of the father of lies. And, since complaining is nothing less than charging God with mismanagement of your life, you've got to rebuke yourself for any and all grumbling of any kind. (Exodus 16:2, 8; 1 Corinthians 10:10). When you catch yourself down and discouraged, feeling sorry for yourself and expressing it in complaining,

you've got to say to yourself in as sharp a tone as a mother uses with a disrespectful child, 'Why are you cast down O my soul?' You take the first step out of the land of the blues when you challenge your negative thinking.

2. Then, *Grace Polemics continues by refocusing on all the reasons grace gives you to be optimistic even though you're in pain and talking to yourself about them even though you may not see any way out of your problem.* You defeat grace discouragement by giving yourself grace encouragement. That's what David did. He gave himself grace reasons for optimism. That's what 'hope in God' is. Maybe he gave himself the grace reason for optimism of reminding himself about the Lord's past help in difficulty. Maybe he told himself, 'The Lord who delivered me from the paw of the lion and from the paw of the bear and from the hand of Goliath will deliver me from the hand of this trouble.'[3] Or maybe he reminded himself 'The Lord's my Shepherd so I don't have anything to fear as I walk through this valley. He's with me. And he's enough.' Maybe he spoke some other truth or combination of truths to himself. But the fact he 'encouraged himself *in the Lord his God*' means he used grace reasons to refocus and engender the optimism he needed to 'get up, lad, get up.' 'The Lord his God' is grace talk. It's saying of God and to God, 'You are my refuge and strength, a very present help in trouble.'[4] Christian, you must do the same in your Ziklag. It's not enough to quench the fiery darts of pessimistic thinking with the shield of rebuke. You must attack them with the

---

3. 1 Samuel 17:37.

4. Psalm 46:1.

sword of truth. You must give yourself grace reasons for optimism. You must rush yourself to grace's MASH unit and allow your wounds to be treated by the surgical staff of Doctors Grace Policy and Grace Plan and Grace Position and Grace Privilege. Put yourself in their healing hands by focusing on their realities. Tie a tourniquet around your hemorrhaging optimism by declaring to yourself the fact that Grace Providence controls what you're now facing and Grace Provision will be more than enough to help you face it well. Apply a Grace Promise antiseptic that's sure to knock out infection by claiming some specific good God has assured you He'll gladly do for you in this situation. And rejoice in the rehab fact that this dismal situation offers you a golden opportunity to make Grace Progress by growing more like Jesus. Believing man, converted woman, fight for the life of your optimism! Fight! Its pulse may be weak but if you have the strong will to see it live and place it in the hands of the Grace Polemics medical staff you'll experience the miracle of seeing it fit as a fiddle in no time at all. Preach grace to yourself. Remind yourself of who and what God is to you. Refuse to call Him a liar. Expect Him to live up to every grace truth He has shown you. Do that and you'll find, 'God is not man, that he should lie, or a son of man, that he should change his mind. Has he said, and will he not do it? Or has he spoken, and will he not fulfill it?'[5] Utilize Grace Polemics and your testimony will soon be, 'Oh, taste and see that the Lord is good! Blessed is the (one) who takes refuge in him!'[6]

---

5. Numbers 23:19.

6. Psalm 34:8.

III. Grace Polemics – the 'get up, lad, get up,' skill of disputing with yourself in your down times and arguing yourself back to optimism by preaching grace to yourself – isn't natural. You've got to embed it in your life. You embed it by disputing with yourself when you're in Ziklag... and disputing with yourself when you're in Ziklag... and disputing with yourself when you're in Ziklag – until Grace Polemics becomes your usual way of banishing pessimism and restoring optimism about God to its rightful throne after a temporary *coup d'etat*.

Strategy number two for recovering optimism about God works. Because it does, I recommend that you *utilize Grace Polemics* to help you 'get up, lad, get up' whenever you find yourself in Ziklag.

19

Strategy *Three* for Staying Optimistic about God: Employing the Grace Pledge

'Every once in a while in the Samson story up pops a reminder of the fact that Samson is God's man, set apart for God's work, and it is God who is overruling the course of Samson's actions and experience. It is this part of the Samson story that gives us hope. We too live tragic-comic flawed lives, lives full of mistakes and deficiencies, lives in which what we think of as our strengths take us ego-hopping and so become real weaknesses. But God was God to Samson. … (and) Samson's God, who is our God, is a God of great patience and great grace. Thus there is hope for us all. Praise his name.'

J. I. Packer[1]

---

1. J. I. Packer, *Never Beyond Hope*, (Downers Grove, Illinois: InterVarsity Press, 2000), p. 31.

A Sunny Place for Shady People

When I finally came under the spell of grace and realized that living a grace-governed life meant staying optimistic about God no matter what, I felt I needed a way to make grace portable. What I came up with is what I call God's Grace Pledge. His Grace Pledge is, *Wherever you are in your story I will give you grace so you can give me glory.* I believe this is an accurate summary of what God pledges in the many verses represented by the following: 'Call upon me in the day of trouble and I will deliver you, and you shall glorify me ... Surely goodness and mercy shall follow me all the days of my life, and I shall dwell in the house of the Lord forever ... Simon, Simon, behold, Satan demanded to have you, that he might sift you like wheat, but I have prayed for you that your faith may not fail. And when you have turned again, strengthen your brothers...For I am sure that neither death nor life, nor angels nor rulers, nor things present nor things to come, nor powers, nor height nor depth, nor anything else in all creation, will be able to separate us from the love of God in Christ Jesus our Lord. ... And I am sure of this, that he who began a good work in you will bring it to completion at the day of Jesus Christ.'[2] Isn't God pledging in these verses to give us grace wherever we are in our story so we can give Him glory? I think He is. And employing His Grace Pledge is the third strategy I offer you for staying optimistic about God. Here's the proposition: *To stay optimistic about God, focus on grace by developing the habit*

---

2. Psalm 50:15; Psalm 23.6; Luke 22:31-32; Romans 8:38-39; Philippians 1:6.

of constantly reminding yourself that wherever you are in your story God will give you grace so you can give Him glory. Let's take a closer look at this habit of employing the Grace Pledge.

I. *Your life is your story.* No writer's block curses you. No blank page haunts you. Instead, you're Shakespeare-prolific as line after line, paragraph after paragraph, chapter after chapter flows from the pen of your choices, decisions, reactions, and responses. By now your manuscript is New York City phone book thick. And you're not finished.

Scary, isn't it? I'll fess up. Writing my story scares me. I don't write well. I find character development especially bedeviling. Still, I don't fear a rejection slip when I'm through with my *magnum opus*. I have the best editor in the business. The Lord God edits my story. Yours, too. And He knows how to write!

Someone asked author Shelby Foote about his writing mechanics: how did he go about the task of putting words on paper? The Mississippi native drawled, 'With an old steel-tipped pen I dip in ink every few sentences.'[3] Ask the Lord, 'How do you go about editing your peoples' stories?' He answers, 'With a love-tipped pen I dip in my grace every few sentences.' Your story, like mine, is a grace story. Ours are grace stories because God promises to give us grace wherever we are. He promises He'll help us. And one of the ways we experience His help is by employing His Grace Pledge. I employ it by quoting it and praying it constantly.

---

3. This quote comes from C-SPAN's Brian Lamb's television interview of Foote broadcast a number of years back.

Allow me to share with you two examples of how I employ the Grace Pledge, one from my ordinary days, the other from my self-made messes.

II. *I quote the Grace Pledge and pray it to enjoy Grace Pleasures on ordinary days.* I'm an ordinary man. I live an ordinary life. Most of my days pass in metronomic sameness. But this ordinary man named C. L. Chase is also a Grace Person. This means God offers me Grace Pleasures as I go through my day. And I am learning to appropriate more and more of them by employing the Grace Pledge. A couple of for instances, one from the other day, the other from today. My wife and I have been struggling over something our neighbors have been doing. A few days ago, I finally decided it was time to talk with them. So about 5:30 in the afternoon, I quoted the Grace Pledge and prayed it. 'Father, you tell me wherever I am in my story, you will give me grace so I can give you glory. You know I need to speak to Harry (not my neighbor's real name). Please let him be in his yard and let me have a good talk with him. Help me to be neighborly in what I say and him neighborly in how he receives it.' Harry was outside and we had a problem-resolving talk. I went inside giving God glory for giving me grace where I was in my story.

Again, tonight I have to speak about one of our graduates at our school's annual Senior Honors banquet. I'll have one minute to say something meaningful about this student. So, I reminded myself of God's Grace Pledge and turned to Him and prayed, 'Father, you tell me that wherever I am in my story you'll give me grace so I can give you glory. I need your grace help to come up with something fitting for my senior. Please help me.' Shortly after that, I spotted and cut a rose from this girl's character garden. I put it in the vase of a paragraph, watered it again with prayer, and plan on giving it to her in about five hours. Then I gave God glory for giving me grace where I was in my story.

These two examples, I give God glory in saying, are becoming the norm for me. My ordinary life is becoming the venue for my extraordinary Grace-God's goodness as I experience Grace Pleasure after Grace Pleasure by employ-ing the Grace Pledge. I encourage you to employ it too.

III. *I also employ the Grace Pledge when I'm in a self-made mess.* I'm sad to say that my story is sometimes darker than a witch's heart. And I'm the reason. In these times I'm like former Alabama QB Kenny 'The Snake' Stabler. He hurt his knee one year, couldn't play football, and quit going to class. Soon this telegram came: 'You are indefinitely suspended from the Alabama football team. Paul W. Bryant.' The next day a second telegram arrived, sent by Alabama's most illustrious former player. It read, 'He means it. Joe Namath.' Stabler was in a self-caused mess. Like the kind Abraham got in trying to save his own skin by lying about Sarah in Egypt; and David got in by Hugh Hefner conduct compounded with mafia hit-man ruthlessness; and Jonah got in by going AWOL; and Peter got in by sleeping when he should have been supplicating[4] – to name just a few of the godly people who were arrested,

---

4. Abraham, Genesis 12:14–13:4; David, 2 Samuel 11; Jonah, Jonah 1-2; Peter, Luke 22:31-34; 54-62.

booked, fingerprinted, and jailed for self-caused messes. I've shared a cell with them. Haven't you?

Humorist Lewis Grizzard says, 'Life's like a dogsled team. If you ain't the lead dog, the scenery never changes.' That's funny but false. Grace is a scenery changer. Grace changed the scenery for Abraham, David, Jonah, and Peter. They experienced grace in their self-caused messes. So have I. Again and again, as I've employed God's Grace Pledge I've found Him helping me *wherever* I am in my story. You'll find Him doing the same for you.

One way God gives us grace in our self-caused messes is by refusing to quit on us. Richard Pitino is the son of basketball coach Rick Pitino. One summer Rick offered Richard a job at his basketball camp. Richard opted for employment at a Kentucky thoroughbred farm. A few days of shoveling something besides hay quickly dispelled the job's glamor. Richard was ready for a career change. He called his dad. His pitch ended with, 'Dad, I just want to come and work at your camp.' Rick understood. Then said, 'No.' Richard was a Pitino. Pitinos don't quit.

Neither does grace. Grace is God telling us, 'Nothing will make me wash my hands of you!' Grace's wedding day vow to us was 'for better or worse … I plight thee my troth.' Even when we give grace grounds for divorce, it never files. Does an emergency room doctor refuse to treat a patient bleeding from attempted suicide? Don't be ridiculous! He's an *emergency* room doctor for heaven's sake! So is grace. Grace is there when you're wheeled in on a gurney, hemorrhaging from self-inflicted wounds, pulse barely detectable, close to flat-lining. Grace's Hippocratic oath is 'I will never leave you nor forsake you.'[5] Even in a self-caused mess God won't quit on you. Are you in one now? Don't listen to Satan. God hasn't given you up. And won't.

A second way God will give us grace in our self-caused messes is by forgiving us the moment we confess. I'm not a computer genius. Best Buy will never hire me as a geek. But I'm a whiz with one computer skill. I'm the Bill Gates of deleting. I get plenty of practice with advertisements slipping over my spam border. Two of the most annoying are for Viagra and Valium. (Yea, I think so too. What do they think they know about me?) When these ads show up I delete them on their merry way.

I say with no irreverence, in fact, just the opposite, with awe: God has a delete button. 'If we confess our sins he is faithful and just to forgive us our sins and to cleanse us from all unrighteousness.'[6] When you confess sin, even the sin of a self-caused mess, the Lord deletes it so completely nothing's left on your hard drive. The blood of Jesus cleanses from all sin! Believe this when you're in a self-caused mess. Defy Satan's lie that you're hopeless, lean not to your own understanding, remember the Lord's thoughts are not your thoughts and His ways are not your ways, and confess and experience again how amazing grace is.

A third way God will give us grace in a self-caused mess is by helping us in the mess. Sometimes His grace will don its SWAT team uniform, kick down the door, and rescue you from the mess. You find Him doing this with Abraham,

---

5. Hebrews 13:5.
6. 1 John 1:9.

Lot, Jonah, and Hezekiah.[7] He may well add your name to this list.

At other times God will leave you in the mess. Like a father pep-talking his just beaned Little Leaguer back into the batter's box to remove the boy's fear of getting hit again – and giving the boy the opportunity of turning the tables by becoming a hitter pitchers fear – the heavenly Father doesn't lift us out of a problem we've caused ourselves. He does something else: He gives us whatever we need to handle things submissively so that we come out with improved character. You find Him doing this with Jacob, Zacharias, and Peter.[8] He may well add your name to this list.

But either way – by rescuing you from your self-made mess or helping you face it in a way that brings Him glory and you good – He will be there with you and for you. Even in a self-made mess you will find Him 'a very present help in trouble.'[9] And the thing to do when you're in such a mess is remind yourself of His Grace Pledge and pray it to the Father whose pledge to you it is.

III. It's always – ALWAYS – best not to sin. No sin is 'little.' Each is what Joseph called 'great wickedness against God.'[10] It's always – ALWAYS – best to follow Moses and

---

7. Abraham: Genesis 12:10-13:4; Lot: Genesis 19:15-16; Jonah: Jonah 2; Hezekiah: 1 Kings 22:32-33.

8. Jacob: Genesis 48:15-16; Zacharias: Luke 1:5-23; 1:57-79; Peter: Luke 22:31-34.

9. Psalm 46:1.

10. Genesis 39:9. Charles Spurgeon reminds us, 'Whatever the grace of God may do for us, it cannot make sin a right thing, or a safe thing, or a permissible thing. It is evil, only evil, and that continually. O children of God, be not enslaved by fleshly lusts! O Nazarites unto God, guard your locks, lest they be cut away

choose 'to be mistreated with the people of God than to enjoy the fleeting pleasures of sin.'[11] Yet fall you may. When your story becomes a chapter about a self-made mess you'll be sorely tempted to despair. Satan will tell you your situation is hopeless. Your own heart will agree. But God won't. Even when you find yourself in a self-caused mess of epic proportions, He *will* not quit on you; He *will* forgive you; and he *will* help you handle it His way.

Somerset Maugham called Monaco 'A sunny place for shady characters.' God's Grace Pledge assures you that's what His grace is when you're a shady Christian. You have His word on it. Maybe even as you read this you're in the shade. You can come back into the sun by reminding yourself, 'Wherever I am in my story, God will give me grace so I can give Him glory' and turning to Him and saying 'Father, I'm in a self-made mess in my story. I need your grace. Please forgive me and either deliver me or help me handle what I've done in a way that honors you and brings good to me.' Do that and you'll see: *wherever* you are in your story, God *will* give you grace so you can give Him glory.

IV. *When you begin employing the Grace Pledge in your ordinary days and self-made messes you find something wonderful happening as God gives you grace: you begin giving Him glory.* Employing the Grace Pledge turns ordinary

---

by sin while you are sleeping in the lap of pleasure! O servants of Jehovah, serve the Lord with heart and soul by his grace even to the end, and keep yourselves unshorn by the world!' Charles Spurgeon, *The Metropolitan Tabernacle Pulpit*, Volume 33, (London: The Banner of Truth Trust, 1969), p. 15.

11. Hebrews 11:25.

living into an adventure that makes Indiana Jones' life seem boring. God becomes real to you. Instead of being someone you chat with for a moment in a Quiet Time, then forget about like a pencil put behind your ear, he becomes so present, paramount, and participatory in your life that you wake up looking forward to what His grace has in store for you today. As you stay in touch with Him through employing the Grace Pledge every day, all day long, you begin enjoying Him. And precious things like joy, peace, praise, thanksgiving, and obedience become daily realities. In other words, as He gives you grace wherever you are in your story, you begin giving Him glory as never before.

Strategy number three for staying optimistic about God works. Because it does, I recommend that you *employ God's Grace Pledge.*

20

Strategy *Four* for Staying Optimistic about God: Practicing Grace Penitence

'Christianity is for weak people just as we are, but we must honor Christ and His finished work by bringing our failures under the work of Christ and leaving them there. When we do less than this, we are dishonoring Christ and His finished work – as though His finished work is enough for some things but not enough for my weaknesses and sin.'

Francis Schaeffer[1]

'It is with a true penitent as with a wounded man. He comes to the surgeon and shows him all his wounds.'

Thomas Watson[2]

---

1. Francis Schaeffer, *Letters of Francis Schaeffer* (Westchester, Illinois: Crossway Books, 1985), p. 115.

2. John Blanchard, *Sifted Silver* (England: Evangelical Press, 1995), p. 216.

Rx: Take as Needed

Former generations called it 'keeping short accounts with God.' This means quickly confessing sin to God. I call this habit of confessing sin the moment you become aware of it *Practicing Grace Penitence*. This is the fourth strategy for staying optimistic about God. I can put this strategy like this: *To stay optimistic about God by focusing on grace, develop the habit of employing Grace Penitence.*

Since this is a strategy I must frequently employ, I think it best to show you how it works out in my life.

I. *I sin.* One of the few ways I'm like Paul is I walk in his Romans 7 shoes: 'For I do not do the good I want, but the evil I do not want is what I keep on doing.'[3] I'm a Dr. Jekyll, Mr Hyde. By grace, I love God and hate sin. Sometimes I'm Joseph resisting temptation with 'How can I do this great wickedness and sin against God?' firmness. Then – sometimes! – the moment after glancing an arrow off my shield, I drop my arm and I'm wounded! Or I foolishly walk on the battlefield without putting on the armor of the Lord and I'm soon bleeding. I sin. I sin in thought. I sin in speech. I sin in conduct. Sin is an everyday reality for me.

II. *I become aware of my sin.* Sometimes I'm immediately aware I've sinned. Like David when he cut Saul's garment, my heart smites me.[4] My conscience tells me I've failed my Lord. Sometimes I sin and either don't realize it or stubbornly refuse to admit what I've done is sin. Then,

---

3. Romans 7:19.

4. 1 Samuel 24:5.

sooner or later, the Lord sends a Nathan who, with prosecutorial finesse, induces me to admit, 'I have sinned against the Lord.'[5] Either way, as I go through the day I experience conviction that I've wronged the Lord in some way.

III. *I confess my sins.* I go to the Lord, tell Him what I've done, and ask Him to forgive me for Jesus' sake. Sometimes I do this immediately. I'm bleeding from sin and I rush to Dr. Grace to be stitched up. Sometimes I'm hardheaded. Like a typical man, I refuse to go to the doctor until I'm hurting so much I can't stand it. But sooner or later, I find myself at the throne asking the Lord to forgive me.

IV. *I don't confess my sins because I fear my salvation will be in jeopardy unless I do.* I'm not on parole. God doesn't handcuff me and haul me back to the prison of condemnation when I sin. I occupy the Grace Position. God accepts me for Jesus' sake. Because of Jesus' righteousness, laid to my account, God continues accepting me even when I do something unacceptable. 'My little children, I am writing these things to you so that you may not sin. But if anyone does sin, we have an advocate with the Father, Jesus Christ the righteous. He is the propitiation for our sins, and not for ours only but also for the sins of the whole world.'[6] Because of Jesus' advocacy, dread of rejection doesn't strong-arm me into confessing.

5. 2 Samuel 12:1-14.
6. 1 John 2:1-2.

V. *I confess my sins, first and foremost, because God requires it.* Even though God has dropped every charge against me, taken me off death row, and assured me He will never subject me to double jeopardy, He tells me to confess my sins to Him. Jesus teaches me to pray, 'Forgive us our debts, as we also have forgiven our debtors.' John tells me, 'If we confess our sins, he is faithful and just to forgive us our sins and to cleanse us from all unrighteousness.'[7] These verses clearly teach me to seek forgiveness through confession. So I confess my sins.

VI. *Next, I confess my sins because they displease my Father.*[8] I spotlight two words here. Word one is *displease*. Scripture's heartbreaking assessment of David's multi-tasking sins of adultery and murder is 'The thing that David had done displeased the Lord.'[9] I find nothing in Scripture to make me believe this assessment doesn't apply to my sins. My sins displease the Lord: they despise His grace; they defy His authority; they dispute His wisdom; and they devalue His fellowship. If one of my children were to mistreat me this way it would displease me. I believe when I mistreat the Lord this way I displease Him.

Word two is *father*. Wrong done to a person is intensified by who the person is. It would break my heart if, in a fit

---

7. Matthew 6:12; 1 John 1:9.

8. 'God doth continue to forgive the sins of those that are justified; and, although they can never fall from the state of justification, yet they may, by their sins, fall under God's fatherly displeasure, and not have the light of His countenance restored unto them, until they humble themselves, confess their sins, beg pardon, and renew their faith and repentance.' Westminster Confession of Faith, XI.5.

9. 2 Samuel 11:27.

of rage, I slapped you in the face. But it would crush me, making me mourn like a widow at a freshly dug grave, were I to strike my wife. The difference? Who she is. Were I to slap her I'd be wronging the one person on this earth who has loved me, lived with me, and lived for me. Slapping you violates social protocol. Slapping her violates sacred love. When I sin I violate a love even more sacred than my wife's: the love of my heavenly Father. When I sin I displease the One who of His own good pleasure heard His Son cry on my behalf, 'My God, my God, why have you forsaken me?'[10] Who He is makes my sin intolerable. It shames me. I *must* tell Him I'm sorry. So I confess my sins.

VII. *I confess my sins because they disturb me.* Psalm 32 is an autobiography of agony. A believer has sinned. He stonewalls his sin. And he suffers internally for his silence. Guilt grieves him. Hypocrisy haunts him. Depression debilitates him. Why? Is this man a spiritual hypochondriac? No. He is a believer with unconfessed sin in his life. I can't speak for others but I'm reading my diary when I read Psalm 32. Like Yogi Berra says, 'It's *déjà vu* all over again.' When I'm aware I've committed sin and don't confess it, I'm kidney stone miserable. It's only in the ER of confession that I find relief. So I confess my sins.

VIII. *I confess my sins because confession, by keeping me close to the cross, keeps fresh my sense God loves me.* Princeton Seminary President Archibald Alexander sent graduates into the ministry with the counsel, 'Young men, make much

---

10. Matthew 27:46.

of the blood of Jesus in your ministries.' Wise counsel for preaching *and* living. Confession helps me make much of Jesus' blood. It keeps me near the cross. The cross assures me 'Christ loved me and gave himself for me.' And Christ's love for me expresses God's love for me: 'Herein is love, not that we loved God but that he loved us and gave his Son to be the sacrifice for our sins.' I need this assurance. It fuels my love for God and makes me want to live for Him. Since I easily forget He loves me, I need constant reminding. So I confess my sins.

IX. *I confess my sins because Father forgives me when I do.* When I confess Scripture it gives me the assurance Nathan gave David: 'The Lord also has put away your sin.'[11] His displeasure dissipates on the spot, gone like the woman's flow of blood the moment she touched Jesus' clothes.[12] My disturbance ceases like the Galilean sea when Jesus calmed it.[13] And Father allows me again to enjoy the pleasure of His company. So I confess my sin.

Some pain medication's prescription is, 'Take as needed.' I believe this is the Great Physician's Rx for His sinning children. Since I need this grace medicine throughout my day, I confess my way through my day. I find this keeps me focused on grace. It keeps me profiting from grace, prizing grace, and praising grace. And this helps me stay optimistic about God.

---

11. 2 Samuel 12:13.

12. Mark 5:29.

13. Mark 4:39.

Strategy four for staying optimistic about God works. Because it does, I recommend that you *practice Grace Penitence.*

21

The *Fifth* Strategy for Staying Optimistic about God: Abounding in Grace Praise

'Gratitude arises from the...perception, evaluation, and acceptance of all of life as grace – as an undeserved and unearned gift from the Father's hand. Such recognition is itself the work of grace ...

Brennan Manning[1]

'Seeing that God continues to do us good, is it not reasonable that there should be a response on our part, that we should continue to do him homage for all his goodness? Does any one day pass in which we do not experience at least a hundred instances of grace at God's hand? Now is it right for us to think that, when we have thanked him two or three times for the great number of benefits we receive from him all our life, we have leisure to occupy ourselves otherwise ever after? Whenever our Lord renews and refreshes us in

---

1. Brennan Manning, *Ruthless Trust* (New York: HarperCollins Publishers, 2002), p. 24.

the remembrance of his goodness, is it not fitting that we should be moved by it?'

John Calvin[2]

I Say Grace

Thanking God at mealtime is 'saying grace.' This comes from the New Testament's word for gratitude. It means 'good grace.'[3] When you say grace you're saying, 'Lord, this meal is grace and your grace is good! Thanks!' But good grace isn't limited to your taste buds. God's Grace Policy with you means you live and move and have your being in grace. This gives you reason to say grace as much as an athlete says, 'You know' in a postgame interview. God expects you to give 'thanks *always* and for everything to God the Father in the name of our Lord Jesus Christ.'[4] G. K. Chesterton got the memo: 'You say grace before meals. All right. But I say grace before the concert and the opera, and grace before the play and pantomime, and grace before I open a book, and grace before sketching, painting, swimming, fencing, boxing, walking, playing, dancing and grace before I dip the pen in the ink.'[5] This 'I Say Grace all the time' habit is the fifth strategy I recommend for staying optimistic about God. I can put this habit like this: *To stay optimistic about God by focusing on grace, develop the habit of offering Grace Praise.*

---

2. John Calvin, *John Calvin's Sermons on Ephesians* (Edinburgh: The Banner of Truth Trust, 1973), p. 555.

3. *Eucharisteo:* Eu = good; Charis = grace.

4. Ephesians 5:20; 1 Thessalonians 5:18. Emphasis added.

5. www.goodreads.com/quotes/12207-you-say-grace-before-meals-all-right -but-I-say/

I. *God wants you to abound in the Grace Praise habit of thanking Him always and in everything.* I say grace is to be your lifestyle. Here are four examples of what's involved in living as the I-Say-Grace-Christian God wants you to be.

Living as the I-Say-Grace-Christian God wants you to be involves *abounding in gratitude for grace usually taken for granted.* Take the mercies greeting you every morning. You wake from a good night's sleep. A day crammed with Grace Pleasures stretches before you. You prepare for it with the conveniences of indoor plumbing, soap, and shampoo. Freshly brewed coffee and scrambled eggs fuel you. A car in your garage waits to take you to your job. All these trade wind mercies blow from the tropics of grace. His 'mercies are new every morning and great is his faithfulness.'[6] Quit taking them for granted. Start taking them with gratitude. As morning gilds the skies, let your heart awaking cry, 'May Jesus Christ be praised.' Greet every day with saying grace! 'Lord, thank You for bringing me safely through the night. I bless Your Name for the good gifts of a shower with Head and Shoulders and Dove body wash guaranteed to make me smell good all day. The coffee in my cup and whole-wheat toast on my plate are nice too. Thanks!' When you begin abounding in gratitude for morning mercies and the other simple privileges lining your day like people holding cups of water along a marathon's route, you're living as the I-Say-Grace-Christian God wants you to be.

Next, living as the I-Say-Grace-Christian God wants you to be involves *displacing grumbling with abounding gratitude as your response to life's fender bender nuisances*

---

6. Lamentations 3:23.

and annoyances. You're stuck in traffic. Instead of fuming you thank God for this opportunity to grow in patience. That's being an I-Say-Grace-Christian. It's 4:45 pm. You can't wait for the 5 o'clock whistle to blow. Then at 4:50 the boss drops a report on your desk. 'I need you to clean this up before you leave today.' The cleanup will take at least forty-five minutes. But you don't frown before your boss's thoughtlessness; you smile before your Lord's sovereignty. You thank Him for this opportunity to become more like Jesus by walking the second mile. That's being an I-Say-Grace-Christian. Your home air conditioner breaks down. The repair bill will siphon half the cash you've saved for six months for that new set of Ping golf clubs. But instead of chafing at the delay in getting the clubs you praise God you have the money to cover the repairs. That's being an I-Say-Grace-Christian. When you begin treating life's minor cuts and bruises with gratitude antiseptic, you're living as the I-Say-Grace-Christian God wants you to be.

Again, living as the I-Say-Grace-Christian God wants you to be involves *abounding in thankfulness in your head on collisions with trials or tragedies.* In the 1945 British election, Winston Churchill's Conservative Party was routed by the Labour Party. Churchill has to vacate No. 10 Downing Street. His wife Clementine tells him, 'This may well be a blessing in disguise.' Churchill harrumphs, 'It seems to be very effectively disguised.'[7] He has a point, doesn't he? Sorrows, disasters, and heartaches are blessings so effectively disguised that looking at them with the naked

---

7. William Manchester, *America, The Last Best Hope*, Volume II (Nashville, Tennessee: Thomas Nelson, 2007), p. 262.

eye makes them seem curses. But you refuse to look at them with the naked eye. You look at them with the eyes of faith. You look at them through the glasses of Romans 8:28. Looking at them this way you don't grieve as those who have no hope. You say to them what Joseph says to his brothers, 'God means this for good.'[8] You bless His name for being too wise to err and too loving to hurt you needlessly. And you thank Him the day will come when you say of this excruciating pain or devastating disappointment, 'It (was) good for me to be afflicted.'[9] When you begin thanking God in your heartaches because of Romans 8:28, you are living as the I-Say-Grace-Christian God wants you to be.

Lastly, being the I-Say-Grace-Christian God wants you to be involves *ever-intensifying thankfulness because of ever-deepening amazement for God's goodness to you in Jesus.* Anne Lamott says the three essential prayers are 'Help, Thanks, Wow.'[10] Applied to grace, the better sequence is help, wow, thanks. God's grace to you in Jesus is His help. The essence of His help is His commitment of all that He is, to making you all He wants you to be. You can't believe He's helping you this way without a sense of wow. Like a husband finding himself loving his wife more after forty-six years of marriage than he did on their wedding day – and telling her! – growing in grace involves an ever-deepening amazement over God's goodness to you – and telling Him, with ever intensifying thanks. When you are finding your help, wow, thanks for what God has done, is doing, and

8. Genesis 50:20.

9. Psalm 119:71.

10. Anne Lamott, *Help, Thanks, Wow* (New York: Riverhead Books, 2012), p. 52.

shall do growing like kudzu as the years pass, you are living as the I-Say-Grace-Christian God wants you to be.

II. There are three reasons why you should be an I-Say-Grace-Christian.

You should be an I-Say-Grace-Christian because *God wants you to be.* Here's one place where you're never in a dark forest without a compass when it comes to God's will. Here is one place where WWJD is clear as the noonday sun on a cloudless July day. '(G)ive thanks in all circumstances; for this is the will of God in Christ Jesus for you.'[11] The Geneva Bible's footnote on this verse reads, 'An acceptable thing to God and such as he liketh well of.'[12] Being an I-Say-Grace-Christian is being something God liketh well. Doesn't this make you want to be one?

The second reason you should be an I-Say-Grace-Christian is *you honor God by offering Him the Grace Praise of thanking Him always, in everything.* You know whether you eat or drink or whatever you do, you're to do it to God's glory.[13] How do you do this in the ebb and flow of everyday living? The Psalmist says, 'The one who offers thanksgiving as his sacrifice glorifies me.'[14] Jesus describes the one leper's response of returning and 'giving thanks' to him as 'giving praise to God.'[15] When you live an I-Say-Grace life you honor God. When you're grateful for what's usually

---

11. 1 Thessalonians 5:18.

12. *1599 Geneva Bible* (White Hall, West Virginia: Tolle Lege Press, 2006), p. 1239.

13. 1 Corinthians 10:31.

14. Psalm 50:23.

15. Luke 17:16-18.

taken for granted, you honor God's generosity as the giver of every good and perfect gift, and His Good Shepherd faithfulness in meeting your needs.[16] When gratitude displaces grumbling, you honor God's sovereignty as the One 'of whom, through whom, and unto whom are all things,' and His wisdom as One who makes no mistakes in orchestrating your life's details.[17] When you thank God in trial's fiery furnace, you honor His love, His compassion, and His power.[18] And when you grow in your appreciation for His goodness in Christ you honor His grace.[19] You see what this means don't you? This explains why God 'liketh well' Grace Praise. Living as an I-Say-Grace-Christian, offering Grace Praise always and in everything, is giving God glory for giving you grace. Grace Praise is God's Grace Purpose. Doesn't this make you want to become an I-Say-Grace-Christian?

The third reason you should be an I-Say-Grace-Christian is *offering Grace Praise always in everything is constantly reminding yourself that you have reason to be optimistic about God always and in everything.* Allow me to hit the nail again: staying optimistic about God is crucial to living the abundant life Jesus came to give you. Abundant living comes through faith and faith is optimism about God. But optimism about God takes tending. The blazing fire burning in its hearth won't keep itself going. It needs constant replenishing with wood from the Grace Paradigm and Grace Primer cords. You've got to return to

---

16. James 1:17; Psalms 23.

17. Romans 11:36; Ephesians 1:11; Romans 11:33.

18. Hebrews 12:5-6; Lamentations 3:23; Genesis 50:20.

19. Ephesians 1:6, 12, 14.

these stacks, pile a handful of logs in your arms, and come and place them on the fire. You do this with Grace Praise. Every time you say 'Thank you Lord' you remind yourself you have reason to be optimistic about God. You take a log off the grace cord and throw it on the optimism fire. And the fire leaps and the wood burns bright, snapping and popping. Being an I-Say-Grace-Christian by thanking Him always in everything helps you stay optimistic about Him. Doesn't this make you want to be this kind of Christian?

III. *This brings us back to the proposition of this book.* God wants you to live as a Grace-Focused Optimist by understanding and using the fact He is determined to get glory from you by giving grace to you. When you live as an I-Say-Grace-Christian you get fresh grace from God and give fresh glory to Him. Then, living as an I-Say-Grace-Christian, makes this grace and glory exchange the rhythm of your life. When this grace and glory exchange is the rhythm of your life, you are living as a Grace-Focused Optimist. This makes the habit of Grace Praise an important strategy to follow to stay optimistic about God. How do you make abounding in Grace Praise a habit? I offer the following suggestions. First, engrave on your heart the importance of Grace Praise by memorizing Ephesians 5:20 or 1 Thessalonians 5:18. Remind yourself of these verses every day, all day long. Second, yoke Grace Praise to every use you make of a truth from the Grace Primer. So, for example, as you engage in Grace Preaching, you thank God for each grace affirmation; as you use a Grace Promise or bow in Grace Penitence say grace by thanking God for each of these privileges; as Grace Pleasures flow into your life, thank Him for each one. Do this and you will become an I-Say-Grace-Christian. Become an I-Say-Grace-Christian and you will stay focused on grace. Stay focused on grace and you will stay optimistic about God.

Strategy five for staying optimistic about God works. Because it does, I recommend that you *abound in Grace Praise*.

22

A Grace Postscript

'I am not what I ought to be. ... I am not what I wish to be. ... I am not what I hope to be. ... Yet, though I am not what I ought to be, nor what I wish to be, nor what I hope to be, I can truly say, I am not what I once was... and I can heartily join with the apostle, and acknowledge, "By the grace of God I am what I am."'

John Newton[1]

'Grace
It's a name for a girl
It's also a thought that
Changed the world
What once was friction
What left a mark
No longer stains
Because grace makes beauty
Out of ugly things.'

U2[2]

---

1. Wikiquote.or/wiki/John_Newton

2. http://www.azlyrics.com/lyrics/U2/grace.html

THE THOUGHT THAT CHANGED MY WORLD

'A satisfied customer is the best advertisement.' That's true. You're inclined to see a movie, read a book or dine in a restaurant if someone gives you a thumbs up. Well, I'm a two thumbs up customer of Grace-Focused Optimism. It so enchants me that my personal mission statement is, '*God put me here to exalt Him and encourage others by practicing and promoting Grace-Focused Optimism.*' Please don't misunderstand. I'm not close to what I should be. After all the time and effort the True Vine and Husbandman have invested in me I ought to be bearing much more fruit. Still, I can honestly say that I'm not what I once was. The caterpillar is metamorphosing into a butterfly. The frog is changing into a Prince. Simon is becoming Peter. Slowly, yes; two steps forward and three steps back, yes; but, honestly, I'm different. All because of Grace-Focused Optimism. I want to tell you how it's changing me in the hope that my experience will entice you to become a Grace-Focused Optimist too.

I. First, Grace-Focused Optimism is *allowing me to honor God more than I used to.* I'll call Martin Luther to testify on my behalf. He says, 'Faith honors him whom it trusts with the most reverent and highest regard since it considers him truthful and trustworthy. There is no other honor equal to the estimate of truthfulness and righteousness with which we honor him whom we trust.'[3] I'll call John Piper to testify on Luther's behalf by explaining why treating God as truthful and trustworthy honors him. 'Trusting

---

3. http://www.desiringgodministries.org/sermons/battling-unbelief-at-bethelehem

God's promises is the most fundamental way that you can consciously glorify God. When you believe a promise of God, you honor God's ability to do what he promised and his willingness to do what he promised and his wisdom to know how to do it.[4] Since the heart of Grace-Focused Optimism is optimism about God – faith in His truthfulness and trustworthiness – I believe even my feeble attempts to live this way give my Lord some standing ovations He desires and deserves. That is, if Martin Luther and John Piper are right. I believe the Bible says they are. Because of this, I recommend Grace-Focused Optimism to you.

II. Secondly, Grace-Focused Optimism is *enabling me to enjoy God more than I ever dreamt possible*. Return with me for a moment to *Chariots of Fire*. When Eric Liddell explains to his sister his decision to run in the Olympics he tells her, 'Jennie, God's made me for a purpose. For China. But he's also made me fast. And when I run I feel his pleasure.' To the glory of God's goodness to me, I can say in the years I've lived as a Grace-Focused Optimist I've felt God's pleasure more than I ever did before. By 'feeling His pleasure' I mean enjoying my relationship with Him. Living with optimism about Him is making Him and His grace real to me day in and day out. It's bringing His help in sweet and sometimes surprising ways, allowing me to taste and see that the Lord is good. Those closest to me – my wife and friends – will tell you I'm not the man I used to be. I know joy and peace more consistently; I handle

---

4. ibid.

trials more effectively; I fight off my blue moods more quickly; and I'm making progress in areas I once thought could never change as even a Sisyphus rock or two have been pushed up a hill and left there. Again, please don't misunderstand: I'm NOT what I should be. But if you had known me before Grace-Focused Optimism you would see in me as big a difference as Jesus made in Legion when He cast out the poor man's demons, clothed him, and put him in his right mind.[5] Because of this, I recommend Grace-Focused Optimism to you.

III. Thirdly, Grace-Focused Optimism is helping me *live more faithfully as a Grace Patriot.* Stonewall Jackson said of his beloved leader, 'Such is my confidence in General Lee that I would follow him – blindfold – anywhere.'[6] You call this loyalty. Being a Grace Patriot means having this kind of loyalty to Jesus. It's what Jesus means by saying: 'If anyone would come after me, let him deny himself and take up his cross and follow me. For whoever would save his life will lose it, but whoever loses his life for my sake will find it.'[7] I make no claim to be among the Lord's mightiest men. I am not worthy to unloose the sandals of those men and women who were faithful unto death. I can only say that optimism about God is helping me to be stronger in the Lord and the power of His might than I used to be. Because of this, I recommend Grace-Focused Optimism to you.

---

5. Mark 5:15.

6. Steve Wilkins, *Call to Duty*, (Elkton, Maryland: Highland Books, 1997), p. 285.

7. Matthew 16:24-25.

IV. Fourthly, Grace-Focused Optimism is helping me help myself with the indispensable practice of *being my own cavalry*. Let me explain. I spent almost every weekend of my childhood from age five to ten in two buildings called 'The Center' and 'The Teche.' These were the two movie theaters in my small hometown. Every Saturday and Sunday I slipped into one or the other of these cinematic oases to escape the brutal heat of our family's dysfunctional desert. Double features (two movies back to back) were the cool waters in each. One was *always* a western. About 50 per cent of the time the western starred the blue uniformed heroes of the United States Cavalry. The climactic scene rarely changed. Settlers were under attack. Death seemed imminent. Then a hope-inspiring bugle blew and over the ridge came the cavalry riding to the rescue. I often need a cavalry. I often find none is around. This means I sometimes have to be my own cavalry and 'encourage myself in the Lord my God.'[8] Grace-Focused Optimism helps me do this. Because of this, I recommend Grace-Focused Optimism to you.

V. Fifthly, Grace-Focused Optimism is *helping me be a Barnabas to others*. Like a garment soaking in dye, you become what you spend time with. That's a fact of life. So I'm not surprised that spending time with the encouraging truths of Grace-Focused Optimism is turning me into an encourager. I rejoice in this for two reasons: one, being an encourager is being like Barnabas, one of my favorite biblical people; two, being an encourager is being someone who offers God's people something they need as desperately as

---

8. 1 Samuel 30:6 (KJV).

a parched man needs water – yet, I fear, rarely get. I believe many believers need mega-doses of encouragement. They need to be around men and women who are optimistic about God. Grace-Focused Optimism makes you this kind of person. Because of this, I recommend Grace-Focused Optimism to you.

VI. Legion wanted to go with Jesus after Jesus changed him. The Lord had other plans. 'Go home to your friends and tell them how much the Lord has done for you, and how he has had mercy on you.'[9] This book is my attempt to tell you how much the Lord has done for me and how He has had mercy on me. I want you to know this because Grace-Focused Optimism is the thought that has changed my world. I believe it will change yours, too, and help you experience more of the wonder of belonging to God. So, you won't mind my telling you one more time: *God wants you to live as a Grace-Focused Optimist by understanding and using the fact that He is determined to get glory from you by giving grace to you.*

---

9. Mark 5:19.

Appendix One

Athletic teams carry a first-aid kit to games. The kit has the essentials needed to handle anything other than a full-blown emergency. Every believer should have a similar kit made up of God's promises. His promises are especially useful in helping us to stay optimistic about Him when we're facing particular needs in our every day living. Below are promises every Christian should have in his or her kit. Using God's promises every day, all day long involves the following five actions. First, understanding that a promise is God's way of assuring you of some good He will gladly do you. Second, by asking yourself in a time of need: 'What has God promised to do for me in a situation like this?' Third, turning the promise into a prayer that asks God to do what He promised. Fourth, expecting God to do what He promises. Fifth, thanking Him when he does help. God keeping a promise is one of His ways of giving you grace so you can give Him glory.

The Promise	The Particular Good God Is Assuring Us He Will Do
James 1:5: *If any of you lacks wisdom, let him ask God, who gives generously to all without reproach, and it will be given him.*	This promise helps us to be optimistic that God will do us the good of helping us act Christianly in our trials. It's also useful when making decisions, etc.

1 John 1:9: *If we confess our sins he is faithful and just to forgive us our sins and to cleanse us from all unrighteousness.*

This promise helps us to be optimistic that God will do us the good of granting us immediate forgiveness for any sin the moment we ask Him to do so for Jesus' sake. It's especially useful when Satan tells you there is no forgiveness for a particular sin because of its frequency or foulness.

2 Timothy 1:7: *For God gave us a spirit not of fear but of power and love and self-control.*

This promise helps us to be optimistic that God will do us the good of helping us stay calm when we step out of our comfort zone. It's especially useful when dealing with a new client, moving into a new location or engaging in any kind of new task.

2 Chronicles 16:9: *For the eyes of the Lord run to and fro throughout the whole earth, to give strong support to those whose heart is blameless toward him.*
('Blameless' = utter dependence and expectancy, i.e. optimism).

This promise helps us to be optimistic that God is always willing to do us good, even when we're in a self-caused mess.

Isaiah 40:31: *Even youths shall faint and be weary, and young men shall fall exhausted, but they who wait for the Lord shall renew their strength; they shall mount up with wings like eagles, they shall run and not be weary; they shall walk and not faint.*

This promise helps us be optimistic that God will refresh and renew us especially in a time of physical, emotional, or spiritual depletion.

Hebrews 13:5-6: *Keep your life free from love of money, and be content with what you have, for he has said, 'I will never leave you nor forsake you.' So we can confidently say, 'The Lord is my helper; I will not fear what man can do to me.'*

This promise helps us to be optimistic that God will do us the good of taking care of us when we engage in obedience that may cost us career-wise, financially, etc.

Luke 11:13: *If you then, who are evil, know how to give good gifts to your children, how much more will the heavenly Father give the Holy Spirit to those who ask him?*

This promise helps us be optimistic that God will do us the good of giving us the Holy Spirit's help. It's to be claimed daily!!!

1 Corinthians 10:13: *No temptation has overtaken you that is not common to man. God is faithful, and he will not let you be tempted beyond your ability, but with the temptation he will also provide the way of escape, that you may be able to endure it.*

This promise helps us to be optimistic that God will do us the good of helping us say 'No!' to our strongest temptation.

Hebrews 4:15-16: *For we do not have a high priest who is unable to sympathize with our weaknesses, but one who in every respect has been tempted as we are, yet without sin. Let us then with confidence draw near to the throne of grace that we may receive mercy and find grace to help in time of need.*

This promise helps us to be optimistic that we are always welcome at the throne of grace. It is a great incentive to pray big prayers.

Hebrews 12:6: *For the Lord disciplines the one he loves and chastises every son whom he receives.*

This promise helps us to be optimistic that God is dealing with us in love even in our hardest times.

Romans 8:28: *And we know that for those who love God all things work together for good, for those who are called according to his purpose.*

This is the panacea promise assuring us that God is determined to get glory from us by being good to us.

Appendix Two
Grace-Focused Optimism Affirmations

I am a Grace-Focused Optimist because through Jesus, God has made me a Grace Person and wants me to live a Grace-Governed life.

I am a Grace-Focused Optimist because through Jesus, God's Grace Policy with me assures me He is always doing me good.

I am a Grace-Focused Optimist because through Jesus, God's Grace Plan for me is to exalt Himself by humbling Himself to exalt me by making me perfectly and permanently happy by making me perfectly and permanently like Jesus.

I am a Grace-Focused Optimist because through Jesus, God has placed me in the Grace Position of remaining acceptable to Him even though I continue doing unacceptable things.

I am a Grace-Focused Optimist because through Jesus, God has given me The Grace Privilege of making much of being His child because He makes much of being my Father.

I am a Grace-Focused Optimist because through Jesus, God's Grace Providence means everything that happens to me comes from Him and for the incomparable good of making me more like Jesus.

I am a Grace-Focused Optimist because through Jesus, God's Grace Provision is always available to help me enjoy the Grace Pleasures that belong to me as a Grace Person.

I am a Grace-Focused Optimist because through Jesus, God's Grace Promises are mine to help me live for God's glory by becoming more and more like Jesus.

I am a Grace-Focused Optimist because through Jesus, the Holy Spirit is God's Grace Power in me, helping me love God by helping me experience how much God loves me.

I am a Grace-Focused Optimist because through Jesus, God will ultimately bring me to Grace Perfection and make me perfectly and permanently happy by making me perfectly and permanently like Jesus.

Because these things are true, I choose to live today, all day long, using God's Grace Pledge assurance that wherever I am in my story He will give me grace so I can give Him glory.

'Whether evangelicals know it or not, their future as a viable movement depends upon the rediscovery of such God-honoring theology.' James M. Boice

TERRY L. JOHNSON

WHEN GRACE COMES HOME
HOW THE DOCTRINES OF GRACE CHANGE YOUR LIFE

When Grace Comes Home
by Terry L. Johnson

How does Calvinism affect the way you view – worship, humility, adversity, outlook, evangelism, holiness, assurance, liberty, prayer, guidance and living faith? Terry Johnson illuminates the practical implications of Calvinism and how God's grace changes every aspect of your life.

ISBN: 978-1-85792-539-5

Christian Focus Publications

Our mission statement –

STAYING FAITHFUL
In dependence upon God we seek to impact the world
through literature faithful to His infallible Word, the Bible.
Our aim is to ensure that the Lord Jesus Christ is presented
as the only hope to obtain forgiveness of sin, live a useful life
and look forward to heaven with Him.

Our books are published in four imprints:

CHRISTIAN
FOCUS

Popular works including biographies, commentaries, basic
doc-trine and Christian living.

CHRISTIAN
HERITAGE

Books representing some of the
best material from the rich heri-
tage of the church.

MENTOR

Books written at a level suitable
for Bible College and seminary
students, pastors, and other serious readers. The imprint includes
commentaries, doctrinal studies,
examination of current issues and
church history.

CF4•K

Children's books for quality Bible
teaching and for all age groups:
Sunday school curriculum, puzzle
and activity books; personal and family devotional titles, biographies and
inspirational stories – because you
are never too young to know Jesus!

Christian Focus Publications Ltd,
Geanies House, Fearn, Ross-shire,
IV20 1TW, Scotland, United Kingdom.
www.christianfocus.com